UNDERGROUND
CHURCH

If I lived in Tampa I'd join the Underground. Seriously. It's the most exciting and thoroughly missional church I've encountered on my travels. The whole missional thing isn't a theory or a conversation or even a paradigm for those guys. It's a way of life!

MICHAEL FROST, author of
The Shaping of Things to Come

What the church in the West needs more than any single thing are brave stories. Theories, methods, and old church metrics run amok, but stories blow through the paralysis of paradigms and give us practices for a new day and a new church. Whenever anyone asks me what I've seen in America that is truly missional church, I always point them to the story in Tampa called the Underground. For years, I've been trying to get Brian to share their story and am thrilled that they have tried, tested, and now are willing to extend their story into the national conversation.

HUGH HALTER, author, founder of Missio,
and US director of Forge America

In *Underground Church*, Brian Sanders brings above ground valuable lessons learned from leading a church that is solely focused on mobilizing people to reach the lost and serve the poor. If you want to discover a new framework for church that doesn't focus on running programs but on equipping people—this book is a must-read!

DAVE FERGUSON, author of *Hero Maker*

The Underground is proof that being led by the Spirit has always looked and felt like creative, innovative experimentation throughout church history. As the Spirit weaves in and out of people's gifting and calling, the result is a diverse, empowered church that becomes an underground city transforming network.

PEYTON JONES, author of *Reaching
the Unreached* and *Church Zero*

This is not your everyday blustery, grandiloquent, church planter saga. Honestly, I have heard too many of those. The UNDERGROUND story is raw and honest—the real deal. Brian Sanders eloquently teaches the reader what it means to plant a church, to flail, flounder, and then to forge a beautiful new narrative of what it can mean become the church.

LINDA BERGQUIST, NAMB church planting
catalyst, coauthor of *Church Turned Inside Out*
and *The Wholehearted Church Planter*

UNDERGROUND
CHURCH

A living example of the church in its most potent form

BRIAN SANDERS

ZONDERVAN®

ZONDERVAN

Underground Church
Copyright © 2018 by Brian D. Sanders

This title is also available as a Zondervan ebook.

Requests for information should be addressed to:
Zondervan, *3900 Sparks Dr. SE, Grand Rapids, Michigan 49546*

Library of Congress Cataloging-in-Publication Data

ISBN 978-0-310-53807-3

Cover design: John Hamilton Design
Cover photo: iStockPhoto.com
Interior design: Denise Froehlich

Printed in the United States of America

18 19 20 21 22 /DHV/ 10 9 8 7 6 5 4 3 2 1

For the first fifty,
for saying yes

CONTENTS

Foreword 11
Acknowledgments 13
Introduction 15

PART 1. BRAVE IDEAS

1. Origins 27
2. A Dream 40
3. A New Framework 50
4. Foundations 69
5. Results 87
   Window 1 108

PART 2. BRAVE PEOPLE

6. Our Culture 115
7. Surprises 131
8. Our Manifesto 151
   Window 2 170

PART 3. BRAVE STRUCTURES

9. Leadership 177
10. Governance 190
11. Sacraments 209
12. Money 227
    Window 3 243

Afterword: A Brave Future 246
Appendix A: The Manifesto 251
Notes 263

FOREWORD

Despite some incremental changes in the Western church, our churches remain marked by a lack of missional imagination, creativity, and advancement. The predominant strategy of most churches continues to be the largely outdated European form of church that accompanied Christendom. In fact, many evangelical churches are stuck in some variation of the church of Christendom brought about by church growth theory and practice. The problem is that these forms of church have harvested all the fruit they could, and we now need to discover a methodology to reach higher up the tree to gather the fruit that has been left untouched. Because of this cultural captivity, we are very much in need of brave leaders to revolutionize the church and break free from our current thinking. Brian Sanders is one such leader, and the Underground Network is the kind of church that is required.

In only a decade, the Underground Network has become an ecclesial structure that reaches the lost and poor in Tampa Bay by planting what they call microchurches—small, missional communities that all usher in God's kingdom in a unique way. I have been able to visit the Underground on several occasions, and each time I've been inspired by this community of redeemed people— all missionaries, all sent—worshiping God as those who have experienced salvation. The Underground represents the genuine, healthy, sustaining movements we need more of. It prefigures other churches, showing all we could do in our stewardship of Jesus's call.

Most of my work asks how the church can recover and activate the idea of the church-as-movement. In *Forgotten Ways*, I explore the six dynamics of movement and how to activate these in any expression of church. The Underground is one of the few expressions in North America that not only tries these six elements (called mDNA) but also thrives in doing so. And following the incarnational impulse, they have found a way to contextualize the elements and make them their own. It is time for this community to be shared with a wider audience and taken seriously as a viable paradigm for church.

Underground Church is an articulation of an ethos, philosophy, and approach that is a movemental form of the church. In the opening pages of the book, Brian catches us up on the history of the movement and allows us to interact with some of their groundwork ideas. Then, he takes us on a tour of the culture of the Underground and provides a glimpse into the life of their missionary family. Each page is enriched with concepts, illustrations, and reflections that ought to provoke questions and contemplation in our communities and churches. Finally, Brian brings us into the backroom of the organization and makes sense of the complex design and systems that govern the community. At the end of each of these divisions, he offers a story about how these principles play out in the day-to-day life of the Underground. It's a thrilling and powerful look at this incredible church.

We need new church models to help guide us into a new future. Without them we are doomed to repeat the same old ideas that can't quench our desire to see a renewed world through the power of Jesus. Something important is happening in the life and ministry of this remarkable movement, and we can all learn from it.

Take up and read!

ALAN HIRSCH
Los Angeles, 2017

ACKNOWLEDGMENTS

Special thanks to Todd Wilson, for all your encouragement and for making the introduction to this great team at Zondervan. To Ryan Pazdur, Nate Kroeze, Matt Estel, and everyone that worked on the book, thank you for treating each manuscript you work on like it is the only one. To my tireless assistants Alisa Rehn and Kathryn Eng, thank you for always seeing the good in the roughest of drafts. Lots of love to our media team, especially Jessie Rajski and Leann Theivagt for your contribution here and for always making what I do a little cooler. And of course, thank you to all the people of the UNDERGROUND, for living creative, brave lives, and making all of these ideas real.

INTRODUCTION

*If you want to build a ship, don't drum up
people to collect wood and don't assign them
tasks and work, but rather teach them to long
for the endless immensity of the sea.*

ANTOINE DE SAINT-EXUPERY

A Creator Economy

Futurist Paul Saffo argues that the industrial manufacturing complex was born on the impulse to overcome scarcity at the turn of the last century. The result is what he calls a "producer economy"— the hero of which was the manufacturer. Eventually these factories became so efficient that they were able to not only overcome scarcity, but to overproduce. As we created and accumulated more than we needed, consumption became the primary impulse. This new era gave us what we all recognize as a "consumer economy," whose hero was the marketer, the one who could convince us to want what they were selling. Saffo actually marks the month and year (November 2008) when the consumer economy gave way to the newest shift, toward free services, social conscience, and creating value with our lives—what he calls a "creator economy." The hero is now the entrepreneur, the artist, and the innovator. The financial

15

crisis and skepticism about consumer systems of the early twenty-first century has given birth to a new sensibility. Scarcity has given way to abundance. People are no longer looking to produce or consume material goods; we long to create.

If we are looking, we can see these shifts in the church too. Saffo's three economies have had profound influence on the church. The producer economy of the early twentieth century is revealed in the idea of mass meetings, fundamentalism, and the world missionary movement. The consumer economy is revealed in entertainment-driven, need-meeting, market-savvy megachurches. And the recent creator economy, which has its own threats and pitfalls, is revealed as more church leaders recognize an opportunity to tell the story of God with how we organize, empower, and mobilize the church. If Saffo is right and people no longer want to define their lives by what they produce or consume, we may be on the verge of the greatest church planting moment in history. Perhaps scarcity will finally give way to abundance in the church and we will become generous with our money, our time, and our dreams. The UNDERGROUND is a product of the creator economy, and more than that, it is an attempt to build the church and to see the kingdom come.

Who We Are

We started the UNDERGROUND ten years ago with some prophetic ideas about how a church should be defined, served, led, and governed. The result is a story of possibility and an invitation for believers and our churches to join the creator economy. As I write, the UNDERGROUND is composed of 201 microchurches (or mission entities)—of all shapes and sizes—in Tampa Bay. Some of these churches are grand endeavors with hundreds of people, paid staff, and a large budget. Others are made up of a dozen people who are picking a fight with a big problem in the name of Jesus. Then there's everything in between. Our diversity demonstrates our philosophy. The UNDERGROUND is a family. We do not tell people what to do, only that they ought to—in Jesus's name—do something. To the casual observer, the UNDERGROUND might look like just another church, but we are actually a collection of churches. We are a practical paradox. At once centralized and decentralized, we are the church, and yet we are made up of individual churches. We have come to prefer the word "network" (a case I will make later), but at the same time, there is a tangible experience of unity that seems to exceed that term.

For a decade now, we have guarded our organizational process, keeping it as quiet and hidden as we could. The intention was to test our ideas in the crucible of real mission and real ecclesial life before taking them public. We wanted proof of concept before sharing our ideas, so organizational shyness has been the operating principle for our leaders and my staff. We have declined interviews and invitations to share what, until now, has been kept secret. At times, I have been frustrated by the quick elevation of a new idea (or a new leader) before it has been faithfully lived or tested. None of the core functions of our organization are historically unique in church history, but the ways we contextualize these core functions of "church life" have always felt like an untested model. I felt ten years was a good length of time to try and test new ideas before confidently sharing them widely with others. Now, I believe we're finally ready to start discussing what we've learned and experienced. It's time to share our story so it might benefit the church as a whole.

Building a new and comprehensive framework for the church is both thrilling and terrifying. I understand why people rest on tradition—the alternative is weighty. Still, other reasons also keep the church leaning too much on tradition. These include a lack of creativity and imagination, perhaps even a lack of courage. Much of what masquerades as innovation in church form and practice is really no more than superficial change. It is disappointing how little creativity in governance and structure I see in the church. Our creativity is often limited to artistic expression alone. Music, film, dance, theater, and communication are all welcome expressions of creativity within the church, but who is rethinking our deeper systems of leadership, accountability, mobilization, and polity?

Steven Johnson, who has written about the secret to innovation and "adjacent possibilities," argues that most innovation does not result from a light going on in the mind, but from what he calls a slow hunch.[1] No innovation stands alone; each builds upon the discoveries and realizations that precede it. Great ideas, then, are the result of using what he calls the "spare parts" available to an inventor. In order to really rethink church, we have to break it down to its building blocks.

The Pieces of the Church

The desire to love someone is inextricably tied to the desire to know that person. When people fall in love, there is a strong curiosity and longing to know everything about the new partner. No insight or detail is too small or insignificant. Likewise, to really love something is to want to know it, to seek to know it. To really know something, you must be ready to take it apart—to reduce it to its pieces so you can see how each fits together and contributes to the whole. This does not mean criticizing or analyzing it to death, but giving it the attention necessary to truly understand it. If you really want to know how your car works, for instance, you might strip it down, part by part, to see what each part does, why it is there, and how everything works together. I believe people should not set about changing the church unless they know, love, and spend time understanding it. That is impossible without looking at its identity, nature, and function.

Before the UNDERGROUND was anything more, it was a

group of people praying for the love of the church and for our city. None of us were happy with the state of the church, and some of us were inconsolably dissatisfied. I will share some of that dissatisfaction in these pages, but I believe we can only be truly prophetic in challenging the church through first loving, knowing, and understanding her. Real prophets love more than they critique. A few months after my first book, *Life after Church*, was published, a former colleague cornered me about it. It quickly became apparent that he had not, in fact, read the book. That did not stop him from criticizing me, though, for what he imagined it said. I remember his smug insistence when he said, with the surety of a mic drop, "I didn't think we could leave the church, Brian, since we are the church." He assumed that amidst my critiques of the church I was saying we ought to leave it.

Had he read the book, he would have known that the argument he was making was precisely my point. When I first started talking about "leaving the church," even before *Life after Church* was published, I argued it was the structures that needed to be left behind in order to build something better, something closer to our convictions. I am not the first person to say this. We are not the first generation to call for change in the church from the place of love and yearning. I never told anyone to leave the church; I told people to leave the structures and programs that masquerade as church. I told people to leave the church of their deep frustration in order to take their place in the true and enduring church.

As I mentioned earlier, if you want to change something and make it better, understanding its components is the first and best step. This is what we did with the "church" as we knew it; we stripped it down to its parts. The UNDERGROUND started with an initial group of fifty people, and one of the first things we did as a group—before we gathered for worship or anything else—was to take one issue at a time and hash out our frustrations and convictions about it. We spent hours and hours debating topics like money, polity, community, evangelism, justice, multiethnicity, authority, and buildings.

By doing this, we stood in the metaphorical garage without a working "church," focused on a bunch of parts scattered on the floor. The process at times was infuriating and at times humbling, but ultimately, it was awe-inspiring. It was a process of discovering the very heart of God and his intention for us. It started for me with a *sense of love* that was more like pity or compassion, but I have come to realize that it is in the putting back together that you truly fall in love. When a great project sits in pieces, it is humble with lovely potential. It's in putting it together, though, that you discover something truly beautiful. The beauty comes, in part, from combining pieces old and familiar with new and fresh elements. The result is something profoundly personal. For us, it was a sense of responsibility and ownership. We can no longer blame another generation or other institutions for flaws in our church; we own it.

To simply inherit a version of church, no matter how inspired its inception, is to fail to be the church in our own generation. I think every generation should undertake this process of disassembling and rebuilding, because it helps to ensure that if a practice is reinstituted it is because those doing the rebuilding believe that practice, whether old or new, is a wonder.

The UNDERGROUND started with no obligations and no expectations other than orthodoxy and our integrity. We ended up with something more similar to traditional church than I ever would have imagined. We take offerings, sing songs, gather on Sundays, preach sermons, ordain elders, and meet in a building. But to us, these elements are different because of how we use them, and now that we've worked through each of them for ourselves, we own them. We came to decisions about these practices as free people. We carry these traditions forward because we have come to see that God is in them, not because of what was done before or will be done again. We have taken the church to pieces and, little by little, have rebuilt a form that we love.

The UNDERGROUND serves leaders and empowers the people of God to do the work and the will of God. We teach and equip, but we do not command and control. We organize and centralize to serve people, never to obligate them. We collect money in a way that serves the whole body of Christ and, most of all, the mission of God. We have a community of creed and covenant, not cultural homogeneity or ethnocentricity. We have established structures that not only remember the poor, but also prioritize them. We give away more money than we use, and we spend all the money we collect without waste, with care and conscience. We include not just a collection of individuals, but also a community of communities. Above it all, we resolve never to do anything that does not elevate Jesus and draw us all—mission and missionaries alike—closer to him. All that we do and all that we want, in the end, is him.

One day, Lord willing, my children will be leaders in the UNDERGROUND, and they will, I hope, take it to pieces as well—not as a gesture of disdain or disrespect, but as an act of love. I want them to know the church as I do and to understand it by seeing its true strengths and weaknesses. Through the process of taking it apart once again, they will recommit to some elements and not others; they will make it better; and they will make it their own. As time passes, the church often loses vitality and purpose—loses her way. We hope that the mystery of the rebuilding work might be a process that helps those who feel lost (like we did) rediscover the church as something they love.

A Story of Experimentation

I think about this journey, in part, as a research project—as a grand missional and ecclesial research project with experiments and procedures for testing. As with any research project, eventually experiments stop and the results are reported. In the academic world, research is published as a gift to that particular field and beyond. That's what I'm doing here, publishing the results of our findings to benefit the fields in the kingdom of God. The very idea behind research and experimentation is to expand the boundaries of a scientific field. The goal is that, as the body of knowledge grows, others can build upon that knowledge and further expand it. In the language of innovation, this sharing opens the "adjacent possibilities."[2] Progress in any field is tied to the process of experimentation, knowledge acquisition, and expansion.

It is astounding that although the church conversation has turned toward mission in the past few years, so many are only now beginning to take the risks and steps of obedience that such a conversation requires. While I rejoice in the conversation and the progress of many, I often feel that both the conversation and the outgrowth of it are lagging behind. We're ten years into our journey as a church defined by mission, and this affords us a unique and invaluable vantage point from which to report findings and to lead further. We hope to do that.

A part of me would like to keep working locally and stay under the radar. I am personally hesitant to propagate anything that resembles translocal leadership. But the result of our decade of practicing revolutionary ideas has revealed things too precious to hold back and too important not to share with the whole body of Christ. In the end, these results belong to us all. And they hold the information and the hope we all so desperately need. Don't get me wrong; it is not that we have not failed greatly along the way. We certainly have. I certainly have. And I will do my best to share some of that failure with you, because that learning, too, is a gift.

Trying to tell a story like ours feels like a daunting task. The story is too complex and involves too many people to ever fully and faithfully articulate. But there are principles that stand out in the telling of our story that will serve to paint a parallel picture, not merely of the UNDERGROUND, but also of the true church. My deepest hope is that you will see in our story the greater story of your own life and what is possible in our time.

In trying to fully appreciate and describe this community, I have discerned three rare elements: courageous ideas, courageous people, and courageous structures. We need all three. The commodities themselves are not rare—ideas, people, and structures—but when they are enhanced by courage and put in service to the church, they are extraordinary. Courage is what makes every healthy and thriving church unique, because it is vital to our lives on mission. C.S. Lewis said, "Courage is not simply one of the virtues, but the form of every virtue at the testing point."[3] So when I talk about courageous ideas, people, and structures, I am talking about the point at which each of these was tested. Our tests and experiments revealed the best (and worst) of all three. In order to tell the story of the UNDERGROUND in a way that inspires, I must describe what these entities look like when courage is applied at their testing point.

For this reason, I have divided the book into three parts: brave ideas, brave people, and brave structures. I am convinced that the possibility for real and lasting change lays at the overlap of these concentric realities.

Jesus looked at the lost world he walked in, and instead of being overwhelmed by it, he saw that there was plenty and urged us to pray for people who could see that bounty and swing the sickle of harvest.[4] The story of the UNDERGROUND is the story of people who have come to believe in that abundance. We see abundance in a world of need because our Father is Creator and Lord, and we are his creative and empowered children. We go because his son, Jesus, who is our teacher and Lord, went before us. His example is our deepest identity, a flame for the soul and a light for the world.

Part 1

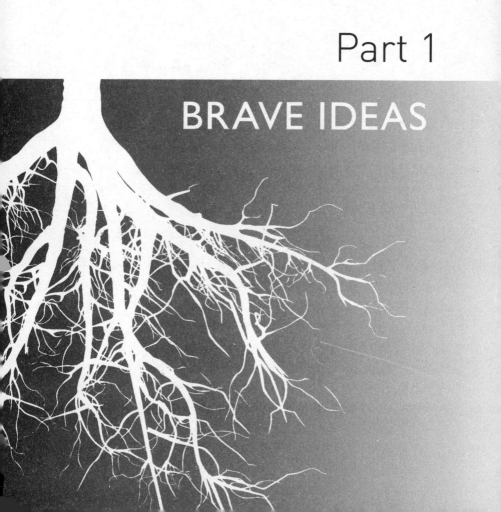

BRAVE IDEAS

Chapter 1

ORIGINS

We are the ones we have been waiting for.

JUNE JORDAN

*T*his is the story of a relatively small but potent expression of the kingdom that has come to understand itself as something unique and worth knowing. It begins with an apostolic story of which I am not the hero, but in fact perhaps the villain at times. Since I was the first mover of this story—or perhaps the first to be moved—it begins with me.

I finished college in 1994, or should I say it finished me. I was twenty-one, newly married with a baby on the way, and ready to start my life in the "real" world. I was offered a job with InterVarsity Christian Fellowship, in the city where I was born, to pioneer work at the University of South Florida. It was one of those ministry jobs that didn't come with much money or many people. It was a chance to start from scratch, so I took it. "It has always been my ambition to preach Christ where he was not known," said Paul.[1] The same was true for me.

The genesis of what we now call the UNDERGROUND movement really began with my first step into the nothingness of that pioneering work. Perhaps all movements start in a similar space. My first real job was a blank slate, and I had all the missionary hope a twenty-one-year-old could muster. I was asked to reach out to a campus and change the world. In the end, I believe this lofty goal must be why I said yes. It was a big enough task, worthy of investment. I stepped onto the massive commuter campus of South Florida with very little knowledge of how to do what I had set out to do. That was important too, and illustrates something very important that I learned in the years that followed—every movement begins by coming face-to-face with a mystery.

My experience of innovation flowered through a process described by Roger Martin in his groundbreaking book *The Design of Business*. Martin argues that all innovation follows a predictable, observable process.[2] First, he says, you start with mystery or what he calls an "impossible question." In the throes of that mystery, you struggle and scrape your way to a series of heuristics or rules of thumb that narrow the answer. Finally, if the heuristics prove true, you find your way to algorithms, repeatable processes that always produce the results you seek.

It is in that first moment, when we are threatened by the vastness and the mystery, when we find God. He is active throughout the process, but he is never more real to us than in the place of desperate impossibility, when we feel there is no way to do what he has sent us to do. Like the children we are, we cry out. If bravado moves us to the threshold, it is prayer alone that carries us into the house. The nothingness of starting something new, I would come to believe, is the essence of discipleship. Recapturing that experience for myself, over and over, and offering something similar to every follower of Jesus that I influence, is the purpose of my life's work.

Campus Soil

I remember walking onto the South Florida campus feeling conspicuous. I was probably suffering some version of what psychologists call imposter syndrome—the feeling of inadequacy and knowing that you don't belong, and that others will find out you are a fraud. I remember standing atop the parking garage, praying and surveying the vast campus, contemplating my impossible task. In my prayer, I considered my limitations and, even if only for a mustard-seed moment, the capacity of God to accomplish the impossible task. That day, I prayed for every residence hall and for a movement to begin.

Unsure of where to find instruction amidst my desperation, I fell headlong into the pages of the Acts of the Apostles, feeling—as all apostles[3] do—the timelessness of the mission of God. Inspired and instructed by the life, community, and witness of the early church, I built a team. Over the course of the next three years, we planted witnessing communities in every residence hall. God used us to build a mission on that campus that grew into something substantial and beautiful.

Urban Soil

Despite the success of that campus ministry, I was restless. I saw in Jesus a cutting edge that challenged everything about our privilege as Western disciples of Jesus. As I continued ministry and mission at the University of South Florida in Tampa, I started taking trips to the developing world to learn more about mission and to witness to the lost. I became a student of revolution and liberation, both political and spiritual. I moved my young family into the highest crime neighborhood in Tampa to be close to the most desperate persons, believing Jesus would also choose to live and serve there. Each of these choices took their toll on me. The edifice of my American Protestantism began to crumble, and I became grateful for the demolition. Picking through the rubble of that inherited system helped me open my heart to the way of Jesus and to the promise of his kingdom.

My family and our growing ministry formed an intentional community and committed ourselves to the poor of our city. I pledged to take university students out of their world and into this other world I had discovered as often as I could. This focus on a larger mission field proved to be a critical feature in the foundation of the UNDERGROUND.

The first program our group started was a tutoring project, followed by a summer-long poverty "immersion project" meant to help university students encounter God in the beauty and pain of an American inner city. I thought of our work among the poor as the discipling of students and not as a mission in itself. To my mind, the students were the mission, the inner city was the classroom, and the poor were the professors. But as our campus witness grew, so did our presence in the neighborhoods. I started to understand more of what Jesus meant when he said, "Whatever you did for the least of these you did for me."[4] We were following Jesus into the heart of poverty. Whenever you look at the anatomy of a revolution, you always see students near the center. There is virtually no example in history of a revolution that was not fueled by the hubris, idealism, and sacrifice of the young. And so it turned out that we were planting the seeds of just such a revolution—rather, God was planting us.

Because I showed aptitude for tilling new ground, I was asked by InterVarsity Christian Fellowship to take responsibility for an unreached area of my state and to hire staff to begin new work on every campus. It was a role I relished. Over the next few years, we started outreach efforts at every major school in that area. It was a time when lots of people were ready to take a job with no money, only the excitement and challenge of that impossible mystery.

Then our students started to graduate.

Frustration

Perhaps every college ministry seems this way to the people involved, but it truly felt like we were doing more than mere "college ministry" during that time. Naturally, this was all happening because I was starting college parachurch groups, but something seemed unique to this project, like we were living out the Lord's Prayer, "on earth as it is in heaven" as we were encountering the kingdom of God in very literal ways and seeing the transformation that comes with it.[5] We were laying down our lives for the glory of Jesus and the coming of his kingdom. We were truly invested, not just in our campuses, but also in the city we loved and in the poor that Jesus said were blessed. While some students didn't give as much attention to their studies as they did to the kingdom, the college didn't mind. When enough credits were amassed, they gave pieces of paper to each of our comrades, and one at a time, our student disciples began to leave college. They had gotten more than just a degree, though; they had a purpose too.

All of a sudden, a new set of demands and pressures fell on our graduates. With school in the rearview mirror, they felt like they had to get real jobs, settle down, get married, buy houses, have kids, and start acting normal. Of all those expectations, the most treacherous seemed to be that they must find a "proper church." Many of these individuals had become Christians through our campus ministries, and all they knew about Jesus and "church" came from these groups. They understood mission, witness, care for the poor, and radical community only through the lens of our work. There was little dissonance between the lives they were trying to lead and the pages of Scripture. Now, they were trying to fit into the middle-class churches that surrounded us.

It wasn't pretty.

Three things happened. One group acquiesced; another group dropped out; and a third group persevered. The pressure to conform to their new church environment, coupled with what Jesus called "the worries of this life" and the "deceitfulness of wealth," caused the first group to give up the way of life they had learned and loved.[6] Most of them would come to recall their time in college as a crazy experience, chalking it up to the exuberance of youth.

Another group simply refused to go to a "normal" church once they graduated. The dissonance, between the Jesus they had pledged to follow and the Jesus preached in the comfortable middle-class churches, was too great for them. They simply could not stomach it, and eventually, they came to realize they didn't have to go to those churches. They still loved Jesus, but they had drifted out of formal church fellowship.

Finally, there was a group who persevered in their church attendance while hating every minute of it. I counted myself in this group. I was still a full-time missionary on campus, and church attendance *somewhere* felt like an entry-level requirement. Even nominal Christians go to church. So, I just complained. Even though no one was listening, that didn't stop those of us in this group from railing against a system with which we could not come to terms.[7] Leaving never seemed like an option.

At some point, we woke to the fact that if we wanted something new we would have to start with the mystery of the unknown. When we are handed someone else's hard-fought algorithm for the church, we miss the process of discipleship that comes from understanding how that algorithm developed. And we are also trapped by someone else's conclusions about what it means to know and follow Jesus. We will all eventually question a Jesus who is handed to us by someone else. We need to experience Jesus for ourselves and come to conclusions on our own. Of course, we aren't starting from scratch; the journey is guided by those who have gone before us. But inheriting a religious system without understanding where it comes from fails to transform us, and it almost never leads to depth in our relationship with God. There is a role for tradition and for learning from the past—these are critical gifts to the church. But in order to be received, they must be offered to the next generation with some flexibility.

We had not experienced the church as something offered or as something with flexibility.

In the end, we did not choose to leave behind traditional forms of church simply because we were frustrated (although at times we were). We left because we were alive with the hope of the kingdom of God at work in and through the people of God. We were not seeing this hope in the churches we attended, even though we played by the rules. We were involved in everything they told us to get involved in. We went to the services, attended the classes, even taught the classes and led the services. But in the end, we could not escape the nagging, burning belief that there was more to the church of Jesus Christ than what we were experiencing in our classes and services. We were not trying to be obstinate or petulant. On the contrary, we had a childlike belief that, in spite of all we were seeing, the church could yet be something beautiful and potent. We believed that something greater was possible.

Hope

Some have accused me of being "anti-church" and an opponent of the church, but nothing could be further from the truth. I believe in the church and yearn for it. Every disciple, pastor, and missionary I know who loves and leads the church shares this longing. We seek the true church and grieve the counterfeit versions that exist, masquerading as the Bride of Christ. While I resist those imposters, I am also guilty of contributing to them. At our best, in our deepest dreams, we all yearn for a renaissance of the church that would strip away the excess to unleash the church in its purest and most potent form. This is part of an ongoing renaissance of the church, something called *ecclesia semper reformanda*, the continual renewal of the church. That's not to say we have it all figured out. We have our own imperfections and shortcomings, but we are also starting to see the realization of God's vision for his church and of his promises, which are available for everyone. We are learning that we don't have to settle for less than being God's pure and spotless bride.

One of the blessings of being involved with a parachurch mission was that we did not have to call ourselves a church. It was strangely freeing. Of course, it was not true—we were the church. We were the people of God on campus. Sadly, the mission component of such a parachurch is what has traditionally distinguished (and strangely disqualified) these types of ministries from being considered church. It is as if there is some kind of ecclesial truce between churches and parachurch ministries: *You do the mission,* churches say, *that we can't or won't do.* They seem to make parachurches promise to not offer the sacraments, and then the churches will send a little money for mission work and not consider them a competitor. It was a gift to not think of ourselves as a church at first, even though we always were, and we probably always knew it.

We came to terms with that thinking by asking ourselves, "What is our ecclesial minimum?" If you strip everything away that is not essential to being a church, what are you left with? The answer we decided on was worship, community, and mission. What makes a group of people a church is that they worship together, are committed to each other, and undertake mission together. We can define a church, then, as a group of people:

- In consistent, devoted, and surrendered relationship to Jesus Christ,
- Totally accountable and connected to each other, and
- Engaged in his mission, making disciples and proclaiming the good news of the kingdom of God.

That is a church. Things like rites, rituals, ordination, sacraments, finance, and governance, while good and perhaps even necessary for long-term health, are not *essential* for a thing to be a church of Jesus Christ. But if we strip things down, these three qualities are absolutely essential.

It is easier to criticize a failing form of the church than it is to embody a faithful alternative. In history, when political revolutionaries win, they are often left dumbfounded by the mechanics of governance. It is easy to stand against something and to see that a way of leading is wrong, but it is much harder to know what is right. People who clamor for large-scale change can identify how the old form is wrong, but oftentimes, they haven't really worked out how things will operate better when they finally take power. It was similar for us. As we were refining our understanding about the essentials of the church, we began to experience a shift in power so strong that it felt revolutionary. We found ourselves dumbfounded by the challenge of creating an alternative embodiment of the kingdom in our specific time and place. Yet, this was our challenge. We had to determine what would be essential to our discipleship and then figure out how to enshrine that into the genetic code and germinating culture of the UNDERGROUND. Instead of critiquing others, it was now up to us, by the power of the Spirit, to live in the light of the convictions we held and to embody the vision of discipleship Jesus had invested into us.

We stopped looking to others for direction or identity. There were no founding documents, no denominational halls of power from which to derive our way of being. There was no one to blame either. The result would be a product of our convictions . . . or a complete failure. It was liberating and frightening at the same time.

Those of us who shared this vision continued attending a traditional church, but we began to shift our focus from trying to change what others were doing to what God was calling us to do, right where we were. There were several dozen of us living in or around the same neighborhood, so our first move was to begin meeting as five house churches. Mission work in our communities was a huge part of our life together, and since we were all planted in "materially needy" neighborhoods, we didn't have to look far to find work to do. We reached out to serve the people around us, and we developed a simple liturgy for our gatherings. We began inviting people—both Christian and non-Christian—to take part in our gatherings.

Those years were formative because they allowed us to experiment. We started with the simplest form of church organization—the house church—and discovered its limitations. We learned that we needed an arrangement that could capitalize on the strengths of a house church, while allowing for something more comprehensive organizationally. We weren't official or formal at this point—we had no name, no established leadership, and no clear organizing principle. But this initial group of house churches was the raw material from which the UNDERGROUND, as a movement, was born.

From the Safety of a Living Room

One night in 2002, maybe two years into this journey, we gathered in our living room and counted about fifty graduates of our campus ministry who were deeply disaffected with the traditional church and looking for something different. We felt a responsibility toward them, knowing that their struggle was in no small part a result of our earlier discipleship. We had taught our student leaders to do what they saw in the pages of the New Testament. We encouraged them to share the gospel, seek justice, and repent for sin (personal and societal). We taught them to hate the evils of racism, materialism, sexism, and consumerism. They learned to love the poor and seek reconciliation in their relationships. They learned to live simply and not pursue wealth as a rival to God. They learned to care about the dynamics of global poverty, disease, and inequity. They learned to love all nations and value each culture they encountered. They learned that a faith forged in mission is a humble faith that holds tightly to a few essential things, but one that does not wield the cudgel of dogma. They learned to treasure the work of the Holy Spirit without learning that might put them into a certain category of Christians. They learned, above all, that in all things we must revere Jesus as Lord.

Yet in the churches they now were attending, they found mono-ethnic worship services that primarily existed to minister to those already in attendance. They saw little to no verbal or practical witness. They encountered decadence, consumerism, and the misuse of money. They saw the institutional repression of women and the poor, along with a racial disunity that mirrored the world. They saw virtually no concern for justice, for the plight of the global poor, and for the challenges of the global church. In spite of all these shortcomings, instead of humility from the pulpit, they encountered dogma and certitude. In the very worst cases, the church they encountered was a place where power, money, and middle-class values were Lord, instead of Jesus.

I recall feeling like I had abandoned these friends, people I had once led and labored alongside. And I realized that we needed something more—we needed a vision.

A Vision without Vision

After coming to the realization that a fundamental change was needed, I went to each person, offering my hand . . . and my heart. All I had in that moment was a notion about building something different and a willingness to invite others to help me work out the details. Every one of them accepted.

I have twice read John Kotter's book *Leading Change*. One of his most compelling arguments is about the importance of communicating vision. Vision drives, and vision unites. At this point, though, I felt like I had no vision. All I had was a burning in my heart for something different. Others shared that longing and signed up to follow where it would lead us. What I offered them was a kind of enterprise, without a singular goal. The truth is, I did not really know what we ought to do. None of us did. So we set out on the journey toward finding it together. All we knew for sure was that what we had experienced in the church to that point did not reflect the fullness promised by Jesus. Our hearts longed for more.

There was no master plan, only a common yearning and the desire to search together.

I recently watched an excerpt from a presidential primary debate in which one of the debaters challenged the opponent, "That is not what you used to say. You have changed your position on that." And I wondered, is it wrong to change your mind? Is it something to be ashamed about? Do we really want leaders who hold the same, unchanging view for the next thirty years, even if they continue to grow and learn and serve? Is it wrong to change one's views? I think this disdain for changing views is part of the hubris of visionary leadership. Like seers, we assume that we are supposed to perfectly divine the future and then lead our people to it. Not only is this problematic; I don't think it's what people *really want* from a leader.

What can we learn from this? I think it simply shows that a movement for change doesn't always need a clear vision at the start. *Sometimes it is best to start with only an invitation to pursue God together.* What united our group in those first days was not that we all knew what we wanted or where we were going, but simply that we could not continue heading down the familiar path. We knew that we wanted something different, something *more*, and it was this shared conviction that led us to unite. We had read the New Testament with wonder, but then looked at our own experience with disappointment.

Our vision, if we had one, was to pursue that *more*, and to do it together. I asked those gathered at our first meeting to commit to a season of corporate intercession and Scripture study. Over the next six months, we met every other week to listen to each other and, in open prayer, listen to God.

That was just the beginning. What happened next was like nothing we'd seen before.

Chapter 2

A DREAM

*Fairy tales do not tell children the dragons exist.
Children already know that dragons exist. Fairy
tales tell children the dragons can be killed.*

G. K. CHESTERTON

We needed direction, so we prayed.

We knew that hearing God with all the noise in our lives today could be hard. Whenever I have a major decision to make and really need perspective, I try to leave for a time. If I can, I'll leave the country. Being in a place where the culture and environment is different helps me to pray and to be open to the creativity of God. It reminds me that I am a sojourner and I am God's, and that wherever he calls me I will go. Leaving also frees me to see some of the indigenous idols unique to our time and place. As Americans, we often imagine that we have an advantage over the rest of the global church. We think that our theology, ministry, and church practices are the best and only way to do things. This is, of course, not true. Not only is the global church larger than the American church, it often avoids one of the idols that plagues our church—the deceitfulness of wealth. So my core team and I decided to leave the country to pray and dream. Not knowing exactly where to go, we were sure only that we wanted to plant ourselves among the poor. Truth be told, the church in the global south is growing, while the Western church is in steep decline. We knew we had a lot to learn from church work in developing countries. Eventually, we felt God calling us to the Philippines.

Learning in the Philippines

We knew that we needed mentors and a classroom to learn and explore new ideas. We were familiar with the type of church planting and church growth that America had to offer, but we knew very little about the apostolic voices in the global church. And so we determined that God had called us to take an extended leave of absence, to live for a season in the developing world. We felt we needed to live among the poor, to ask them to "tutor" and teach us how to re-form the church in a way that aligned with the vision of Jesus in the New Testament.

As we prayed, I heard the names of three world cities. We decided to visit each one, and a small team accompanied me as we prayed and asked God to lead us. In each city, we met remarkable leaders and witnessed what it would be like to live, labor, and learn there for a season. Then, through a series of events and prophetic words, we sensed God choosing for us the city of Manila, the capital of the Philippines. There was something about the way the church planters, who we met in the slums, effortlessly reconciled both evangelism and justice, care for the body and the soul, that convinced us. So, in the fall of 2006, a group of us rented out our homes and took leave from our jobs to move to the Philippines. There were nine adults and ten children altogether. I found a row of small apartments in the slums in Quezon City (the largest and most populous city in the metro Manila area) that would become our home for the next nine months. Our intention was to live and serve alongside the poor and the church leaders who ministered to them. We connected with two well-respected Filipino mission agencies, one that did church planting among only the urban poor—their mission articulated was "a church in every slum"—the other that worked directly with women from the sex industry.

Our intention was to live as quietly as possible among the people and to not be a burden to our hosts. Our days consisted of working alongside the missionaries in the slums, homeschooling our kids, and navigating the day-to-day experience of living in another country. At night, we would sneak away from the ruthless Filipino heat to dream, debate, and begin writing the framework and core documents for this new expression of the church. We made notes on everything from governance to centralization, from theology to the use of money, from discipleship to justice, and we collected all that data for the future.

The team members who had remained in the States had committed to keeping a twelve-hour-a-day prayer watch. And our team in the Philippines joined them in this, setting aside one small room in our apartments for the work of prayer, each of us taking turns to cover our twelve-hour prayer watch. Our inspiration was the Moravian missionary practice of the eighteenth century. Because there is a twelve-hour time difference between the Philippines and the United States, our small community of about fifty people was able to keep a twenty-four-hour prayer watch for most of the nine months we lived and listened in Manila.

It was not easy to think, discuss, and plan through the fatigue and heat, but we were strengthened by a Spirit-inspired resolve to see the world differently. There wasn't a single day when we didn't feel grateful for the strength and resolve of the Filipino church. They inspired us.

We remained in Manila for nine months, which gave us time to grow and change. These nine months gave birth to a new understanding of the church, something to which we felt we could give our lives.

The Manifesto

Of all the documents produced during this time, there is one that embodied the burning in our hearts. We called it "the Manifesto." The Manifesto is a collection of the values that summarize what God revealed to us during our time together in the Philippines. The key to this Manifesto and the values contained within it is that it was a product of our work together, not a pre-fabricated vision. These are the values we worked out as a community, and they would drive the leadership of our new organization. These values continue to represent our standard, though we allow for multiple ways of expression. The Manifesto became order in our chaos. While some of the document is doctrinal, it is best characterized as aspirational. Much of what we valued then was not yet actualized in our lives. It represented the change we hoped to see. The Manifesto was and is precious to us because it gave voice to our yearning, not just our doctrine.

Being part of the church of Jesus is not simply intellectual. It is not a group of people who simply believe something (faith), neither is it a group of people who simply do something (works); rather, we are essentially a collection of people who desire something. The faith and works come from that desire. What makes us a part of the church is not the act of believing something, or even doing something, it is yearning for something. More to the point, it is yearning for someone.

The refrain of the church is and will always be, "Jesus Is Lord." Our Manifesto represents our desire to revere Jesus as Lord, and it is both a statement of belief and a statement of intent. We believe it to be true, and this is how we want to live because it is true. These values represent the announcement of the kingdom of God and our best attempt to articulate that kingdom vision for the church today (see the Manifesto, Appendix A).

The Poor

One of the reasons we felt we needed to leave the United States to find new ideas was because we wanted our church to represent God's heart *for* the poor. We spent some time wrestling over that preposition—the word "for." We knew that trying to plant a church *of* the poor would mean that we would likely be excluded, unless we followed the Franciscans in taking a vow of poverty. In the end, we resolved to make this a church *for* the poor (and not *of* the poor) because we believe poverty to be something evil, something to be overcome, and not something we wished to expand or to hold up as a goal. We also considered what it meant to be a church *with* the poor, and while this was a more compelling choice than a church *of* the poor, we saw that if we embraced this mentality, we would need the poor to join us before we could live out our values. We wanted a church that could reach all kinds of people from every social context. We wanted teachers to reach teachers and athletes to reach athletes and doctors to reach doctors. The wealthy need the kingdom too. So we decided to be a church *for* the poor, but not to the exclusion of others.

We identified as sent people, called to plant the kingdom of God in every conceivable corner of society. Every missionary context creates a margin—those who are excluded or even despised. We believed that every one of us was responsible for the mission *and* for the margins of the places to which we were being called. This concept meant a new level of saturation and potency in the churches we hoped to plant. We had seen plenty of emphasis on church planting in the North American church, but we felt that what was being planted was not potent enough, not radical enough to actually do what the church is called to do and to be. The church in America was planting gatherings, but they were not accomplishing the mission of Jesus. For the most part, they were not doing what he came to do or being who he calls us to be.

In the Gospel of Luke, chapter 4, we see that Jesus was reading from Isaiah 61. But he was not just reading a random part of Scripture. Jesus was declaring the primary intention of his ministry: "The Spirit of the Lord is on me, because he has anointed me to proclaim good news to the poor."[1] For us, that primarily means the materially poor, but whatever you make of the meaning of the phrase "good news to the poor," its prominence in the life and ministry of Jesus is clear. We see this throughout the gospels and in the book of Acts. The ministry of healing the blind, lame, and sick, among others, is a ministry to the poor.

And it doesn't end with Jesus. If you read Luke and Acts side by side as a two-volume work, you can see that the declaration of Jesus's intent in Luke 4 is later mirrored in the story of the Spirit anointing the church in Acts 2 and 3. The journey and mission of Jesus in Luke is reflected in the journey and mission of the church in Acts. The revelation: Jesus's stated mission—to bring good news to the poor—has now become ours.

The Good News

Jesus said that he came to bring good news to the poor. Later, he commented, "It is not the healthy who need a doctor, but the sick."[2] Jesus chose the poor because they are often desperate and aware of their need for help; you cannot enter the kingdom of God cloaked in self-sufficiency. "Blessed are you who are poor," he said, "for yours is the kingdom of God."[3] Jesus reminds us that, if we want to see God, we must embrace the work and activity of God, which is available to those who are desperate for him.

The church must embrace the core work of ministry to the poor if it hopes to maintain both vitality outside its gatherings and the presence of God within them. Inclusion and care for those who are poor and marginalized is not just a box that churches need to check, it is a defining practice that reflects our deepest understanding of the good news. The gospel is predicated on the revelation of our own poverty, and the materially poor remind us not only of that, but also of the ever-present need in the world. As long as there is poverty, there is a need for the church. If we build churches that exclude the poor, we risk losing our grip on the reality and power of the gospel as good news for those in need. This is yet another way we came to discover that the poor are a gift to the middle class, because they magnify the deepest truths of the kingdom.

The Mission

Because we had all already been committed to mission and the missionary life, we were very aware that sometimes mission finds itself divorced from intimacy with God. We wanted to embrace mission (task) but also not neglect intimacy (relationship). The mission of the church is more than just outward obedience to the ways and teachings of Jesus. It is a matter of heart-change, and it requires the development of intimacy in our relationship with God and, for that matter, each other. Mission should flow from intimacy and intimacy from mission. They need each other. If we grow in our knowledge of the God we worship and hear the tender whisper of his voice, we will begin to sense his grace for us and feel compelled to do his work. "For the Son of Man came to seek and to save the lost."[4] We knew we needed to recapture the nonnegotiable nature of our missionary identity. So the question was, What form or church structure would enable us to do this? We needed something that would engage every single person in mission.

We began to dream of a church that would do what Jesus did, albeit imperfectly, while basking in the presence of God. We dreamed of a church where everyone was engaged—not just a select few. We dreamed of a church of *missionaries*—not isolated or formalized, but deeply in love with Jesus and equally as connected to each other. When we would gather to worship, it would be a gathering of the sent ones of God.

We imagined a church more like Antioch than Jerusalem.[5] Antioch was a city of prophets. It empowered and released the likes of Paul, Barnabas, Mark, Lucius, and Silas. It was the launching point of the earliest missionary journeys of the church. It is likely the community that led to the writing of the gospels of Mark, Matthew, and Luke.[6] It was a church that discipled Paul and may have helped him to develop the revolutionary doctrines and teachings that would later become the basis of his missionary work. It was a community of freedom and fresh revelation, the first city known for including Gentiles.

All of this was in contrast with Jerusalem, which struggled with ethnic diversity and failed to engage in cross-cultural missionary work unless prompted by persecution. In Jerusalem, it proved difficult to integrate those who had previously been excluded from the household of faith.

We wanted to be a new expression of the church of Antioch, something that would include, serve, and empower the poor, while challenging and blessing the middle class. Our time in the Philippines had been marked by the revelation of mutual dependence with the poor. It was a lesson we did not want to forget. Here is an excerpt from a letter I wrote as we prepared to leave Manila and return home:

> There are things that I know because I have studied them, there are things that I know because I have seen them, and then there are things that I know because I have experienced them. We have grown exponentially in our understanding of what it means to love, serve, and walk beside the poor. We are still far from truly understanding the despair and dehumanization of poverty. But if there is one thing that the Filipino poor

have taught me, it is how much they have to offer me. Those who work with the poor understand what has been called "the riches of the poor" and, in turn, the poverty of the rich. The great tragedy of injustice is that the poor need the resources, freedom, and access that the rich possess, and the rich need the intangible life of faith, generosity, and sacrifice that the poor possess. We need each other.

There is a kind of ministry done among the poor that is defined by our own self-sacrifice. But from living among the poor, I have come to realize that we need them as well. We gain as much as we give. Our call to work *for* the poor is no call to martyrdom; it is hard, but it is also better.

People who rush to work among the marginalized because they have heard a call to martyrdom do not last. It is the ones who come in search of the fullness of life, the grace of God, and the face of Christ Jesus who make it. We find these gifts in abundance in the place of mission.

We left Asia confident that the call to come and die is ultimately a call to come and live. And we felt ready to offer that call to others with a smile on our faces and hope in our hearts. Our dream was of a church encountering Jesus on the margins, and of a world whirling from being loved so fiercely by a church on fire for God.

The Name

One thing remained—*what should we call this thing?*

Before we left for the Philippines, I was working on a graduate degree in London and spending much of my time on the subway system—the London Underground. The Underground is a city beneath the city, something vital to the functioning of the metropolis, essential to its life and operation, yet almost imperceptible from ground level. The ubiquitous signs are the only things that betray the existence of this invisible network of lines to the city it connects and empowers above.

I love that something so important and necessary to daily life in the city serves its role invisibly rather than being the focus of attention or a destination. The London Underground is powerful, yet that power is exercised in service to the people who utilize it. And while the underground subway moves everyone, rich and poor alike, it especially enables the working-class poor to reach beyond the poverty of their own neighborhoods. The Underground even serves to bring disparate classes of people together, uniting them for a time as they share a ride to a common destination. And it does most of its work without much fanfare or attention.

We knew this image—of an invisible, interconnected, powerful network that served the needs of people—represented our dream for the church. My only reservation was that the term had often been used throughout church history. The underground church is already known, frequently as a remnant of the larger body of Christ that has been driven underground by persecution or by threat. It was our wish to honor those brothers and sisters, and so we chose to call ourselves the UNDERGROUND in homage to them. I blush at those comparisons, but I still welcome them, not because I believe we deserve such affiliation, but because we honor them. We want to represent to the world a church that resists in loving protest, pointing people to something greater.

The name represents the embodiment of our practice and our presence in the world. We knew that in choosing such a radical name—one associated with the persecuted church—we would need to back up our lofty goals and dreams with real change and transformation. The framework we had yet to develop would have to be as radical as the name to which we aspired. That was the next journey for us, one that would be filled with great joy and many challenges along the way.

Chapter 3

A NEW FRAMEWORK

What makes a hero? Courage, strength, morality,
withstanding adversity? Are these the traits that
truly show and create a hero? . . . Who are these
so called heroes and where do they come from?
Are their origins in obscurity or in plain sight?

FYODOR DOSTOYEVSKY, *NOTES FROM UNDERGROUND*

The first supersonic commercial airline launched in 1976. It was called the Concorde and was an aeronautic marvel that topped out at more than twice the speed of sound and represented an unprecedented financial and engineering collaboration between the governments of France and England. Even though the Concorde could make the trip from New York to London in less than three hours, the plane could only hold about 100 passengers, and the operational costs were immediately prohibitive. Keeping the Concorde in service cost both governments billions, yet despite its lack of viability for commercial air travel, the Concorde kept flying for twenty-seven years. Why? Because those who had developed it had already invested so much into it that they were unwilling to admit failure and close shop.

The Concorde is the quintessential example of a phenomenon behavioral economists call the "sunk cost" bias. If you open the Oxford dictionary today, you'll even find the term "Concorde

Fallacy," which refers to continuing pursuance of a failed idea or project so as not to waste the resources that have already gone into it.

Much of the way we "do" church today is the result of a Concorde Fallacy. We continue doing what we've always done because it would be too painful to shutter the operation, admit that it has failed, and lose much of the effort put into the endeavor. We may look at the twenty-seven years of Concorde operation losses and struggle to see why generations of government officials would maintain these losses with no returns. Some of it can certainly be attributed to pride. Once we go "all-in" on a model or commitment, it becomes increasingly difficult to admit we made a mistake. Yet, that is exactly what we have to do if we want to turn the ship around. Looking back, we admire the courage of those brave souls who, in 2003, finally took the Concorde offline.

We don't always feel the same way about those who try to change the church.

When our group started tinkering with the broken structural assumptions of the church, we were immediately conscious of a sunk cost bias. There were ideas that made very little sense in light of the mission Jesus had given us. We asked ourselves, *Why was the church operating in such self-defeating and even unbiblical ways? Why were some practices never challenged, even though they were ineffective and, in some cases, unbiblical?* We began confronting our assumptions and identifying where our own sunk cost biases existed. This was the first step toward making changes, and it is often the most difficult part for those who are operating within existing church structures. When you have invested enormous emotional and financial resources into the prevailing framework, change comes hard. Courage is needed to do what must be done.

Instead of beginning with our framework at the UNDERGROUND, I want to start by identifying and describing the prevailing framework of most churches in North America today. When I say framework, I mean the deeper unseen structures and assumptions that hold up the church in its current form. Think of the framing of a house. You can cover it with walls, paint, and art, but the walls are where they are because of the frame. There are strengths to the prevailing framework, but taken as a whole, this framework has failed the essential work of mission mobilization and individual and community transformation. At the very least, the framework that exists must be questioned, preferably without fear and malice toward the possibility of change.

The Prevailing Framework: A Hospital for Sinners and a School for Students.

The prevailing framework for the North American church today is almost entirely focused on the health and development of the people who attend it. Even attractional churches, which make evangelism central to their ministry, still see the visitor as a sinner to be rehabilitated or as a mind whose ignorance needs to be dispelled. We have perhaps overemphasized the idea that the church is a hospital for sinners. Because we have overestimated the power of the intellectual to do spiritual rehabilitation, we also operate a lot like a school, operating under the assumption that everything that is wrong with us can be taught out of us. Under these assumptions, the church is made up of its people, who are sick and unhealthy. Its leaders are the experts who offer a treatment plan, followed by helpful advice, educating us on how to stay healthy. The infrastructure is centripetal, drawing people inward. The leaders—the experts—are primarily focused on gathering, educating, and meeting the needs of those who are wounded and unwell so they can be healthy again.

One strength of the prevailing framework is the ability to exercise control over things like doctrine and the content of what is communicated. If the endgame of our mission is educated people, then this model seems effective in accomplishing that goal. Churches draw people into an educational environment to learn things like ethics and life skills. This framework has a bias for theory, not practice. It struggles to create meaningful community and largely fails at the work of mobilization. What it does well is to create an environment where gifted, higher capacity people do most of the work of ministry, meeting the needs of the rest.

Let's consider some of the *unintended* implications of this framework.

Identity. The prevailing identity of the people who participate in this model is that of sheep—sick and uneducated sheep. Very little mission is done when this is the primary identity of a church. The image of members as sheep—even though it is biblical— tends to imply that people are dumb, lost, prone to wander, and untrained—even *un*trainable. It can be self-fulfilling and lead people to see themselves as immature, inadequate, and unable to do much of the "real" work of ministry. While this biblical metaphor is fair, it is also inadequate, and when it is not balanced with other biblical metaphors, it threatens a fuller understanding of who we really are as people of God.

Operating Model. The model that underlies this framework is a process from *gather* to *teach* and then *serve the 80 percent*. In this model, leaders function as though their role is to tend to the needs of the sheep and to keep them from leaving or wandering. If the people are dumb sheep, then we don't want them scattered. We need to keep them gathered so they can be led, instructed, and cared for by the shepherd. Since this is a biblical image, there is obviously truth to it. People do need care and guidance and teaching. The problem is that we've taken this one identity too far, to the exclusion of other identities and models for the church. Our primary work has become gathering sheep for the purpose of teaching them basic moral theology, ethics, and acceptable biblical behavior. The oft-unstated goal is behavior modification for the purpose of self-improvement.

Again, there are some advantages and efficiencies to this model. It allows the expert leader or shepherd and their team to do all the work of ministry in one place. The infrastructure must be centripetal so that the people with the most skill and acumen can meet the needs of those under their care. And it is inevitable that the building will be central to the work of the church. Today, these buildings are mistakenly called the "church" because all the essential work of the ministry—primarily done by paid clergy—is done there. Needs are met in this framework, but the scope is severely limited by the space and the number of staff and credentialed volunteers. Further, the needs that are met are almost exclusively those of existing Christians.

The heroes of this model are the larger churches. The greater the church's seating capacity, the greater its impact. If the point is to give the sheep access to a master shepherd, then the more sheep the merrier. The bigger the classroom, the more successful the church is. In this model, you will always have a minority of people who distinguish themselves and want to be more involved. The prevailing model tends to put these overachievers to work gathering more sheep.

The 80/20 Rule

Late in the nineteenth century, Italian economist Vilfredo Pareto concluded that 20 percent of landowners in Italy owned 80 percent of the land. On its own, that reality would not have been remarkable, but it was his second revelation that got him thinking: 20 percent of his peapods produced 80 percent of the peas in his garden. The concept that 80 percent of results or effects come from only 20 percent of inputs or causes is known as the Pareto principle.[1]

I first heard of the Pareto principle (also called the 80/20 Rule) in reference to how 20 percent of people in churches do 80 percent of the work. I would later come to also make my own—not so scientific observation—that about 20 percent of givers fund about 80 percent of the budget.

I've since often heard this idea being used to argue various positions, almost always having something to do with productivity. Cutting across disciplines, the Pareto principle seems to apply in nature, social systems, economics, and possibly even psychology, which made me think of the church: *What is the potent minority? If there is such a thing, how can I stimulate, reward, and generally nurture the growth of that minority?* Confronted with the hard reality of the prevailing model of church, I could see that the most productive 20 percent of the church was being used to serve the least productive 80 percent.

Since the prevailing model keeps the congregation in need of its teaching and gathering, and thereby validates the church's existence, church leaders often are unsure about what to do with the productive minority. So, in my experience, those people are put to work inside the church. This means that the most potent and apostolic people are either rejected or repurposed for some internal project, instead of being utilized for outward mission. Our most effective missionaries, I started to realize, were being distracted and underutilized by a system that maintains a large power distance between clergy and everyone else. We started to ask ourselves, *What if we built an organization that was not just fueled by the 20 percent, but one that actually existed for and was run by them?*

A Missionary Framework: The Church Is an Incubator for Sending Missionaries.

Church is made up of its people, who are all apostles (missionaries); its equippers, who are servants; and its infrastructure, which is centrifugal (moves outward). Equippers need, therefore, to help, empower, and pledge to meet the needs of those who meet the needs of others.

The strength of a missionary framework is in its reach and impact. Because the endgame of the kingdom is to see the whole world know the gospel of the reign of Jesus, we need a more radical (and somewhat riskier) structure than a sheep pen. Though sheep are one image for the people of God, there's more to who we are. The missionary framework does not ignore the need for individual development and care, but it does factor in the work of the Holy Spirit in the life of a believer. This framework moves the Christian leader or pastor from the central role as master teacher to a peripheral role as servant and co-laborer in what the Father (through his Holy Spirit) is already doing in each member of the family. Consider what this framework can do and, as he is doing among us now, what he *has done.*

Our Identity as Missionaries

There is no higher honorific in the New Testament for a follower of Jesus than *apostle*. While the term is often reserved for the first twelve disciples and, then later in the early church, for the office of apostle (Eph. 4), I still think the term has value for us all. Just as some are called to be evangelists, we all do the work of evangelism. Just as some are called and operate in the prophetic, we can all hear and speak the Word of God to each other. There is a beautiful shift in each gospel narrative where the writer stops referring to Jesus's followers as his disciples and begins to refer to them as his apostles. This occurs once they have been sent.

No one living in our time would claim to be one of the twelve, but we do see ourselves as disciples. Because we have all, in the story of our own redemption, heard a call to follow him. And we have said "yes" to that invitation. Similarly, as we mature in faith, we will also hear his call to go, and when we say "yes" to that, we expand our understanding of our role and identity from disciple to apostle. I understand that some will struggle with applying that term to all of us. So, if it makes you uncomfortable, feel free to say missionary. What I mean by it is that we're all "sent ones." Both words translate as "sent" ("apostle" is a Greek derivative, and "missionary" is a Latin one). I personally like "apostle" because it carries a certain gravitas, which is precisely the point. Not only does this term identify us as people who have been sent by Jesus, it also carries with it weight and honor—two gifts that should not belong only to people who stand on platforms or behind pulpits.

Unlike sheep, apostles are filled with grace and power. I believe this image is nearer to the way Jesus thought about and described his followers. They were, of course, sinners, and they may have preferred being called disciples, but the New Testament rightly renames that initial band of followers "apostles" because Jesus gave them authority and mission. We are sheep, yes, but we are not merely sheep. We are all stubborn and prone to wander, and we are all in need of the good shepherd. But when one metaphor eclipses all our self-understanding, we have a problem.

When Jesus used the sheep metaphor, he was almost always referring to people untouched by the kingdom.[2] His phrases like "the lost sheep of Israel" and "sheep without a shepherd" imply a need for missionary engagement, not corralling. If they are sheep, they are sent sheep that become shepherds. He did not see them in need of protection, but as fierce, fearless people who would willingly expose themselves to danger. He was not giving them license to hide in the flock. "I am sending you out like sheep among wolves."[3] Unlike mere sheep, Jesus saw his disciples as gifted, called, destined, filled, and adequate. Those of us who lead need to remember that, through the promise and presence of the Spirit of Jesus inside each of us, there is also the promise that his invisible work will mature and equip his people for mission.

The Model of Empowerment

On at least two occasions, according to the gospel records, Jesus sent teams into towns to do the work of ministry.[4] This was not limited to only the twelve apostles, either. Armed with the promise and power of his name, they saw the miraculous. If we are called and sent by Jesus, then the work of church leaders must be to help people discover and respond in faith to that call. The UNDERGROUND knew we had to build something that affirmed that every Christian in every context is being called by God to proclaim the coming of his kingdom. Our work, then, should be to help people listen to and obey that call. For those who have already heard it, our job is to give them permission to pursue their call with abandon.

The same work Jesus gave those missionary pairs continues today. They were asked to heal the sick, cast out demons, and preach the good news of the kingdom. This, too, is our work. We have come to see that every believer has in them some unique and specific call to do one or all of those things. Our leadership exists to remind people of the authority that has already been given to them to comfort those who suffer from every kind of sickness, to help those who suffer under the oppression of evil, and to share the good news of Jesus, his cross, and his kingdom.

Convene Covenantal Community

Once people within our influence understand their calling, we connect them to collaborative communities of people who share the same calling. None of us is sent alone. Finding those who share our calling is a real need. A primary responsibility of the centralized expression of the church should be building community around calling—helping people find each other and forging serious bonds that will carry them through what will certainly be a fiery ordeal. Gathering people inside church buildings to teach them is safe;

scattering people on missions to confront and defy the demonic and the entrenched systems of this world is both risky and daunting. And while the promise of the presence of Jesus always goes with the apostle, so does the grace of the body of Christ.

The place where we most need each other is not in the house of worship, but in the crucible of mission. For the UNDERGROUND, the work, therefore, of the overseer and the centralized church is to offer love, community, support, and accountability for those who go. The centralized church also sets a certain moral and practical standard for leadership. People who are sent to represent Jesus ought to be held to a higher standard of conduct and character. Ensuring that this happens is one of the primary jobs of leaders in this missionary framework. (I talk more about this in chapter 12.)

Serving the Mission

In the prevailing framework of the church today, leaders are constrained to serve only those who come into their ministry sphere—their church building or programs. The ministry, then, is limited to only their capacity and the capacity of that sphere. This also means we are often chasing our tails trying to serve people who are disinterested in the kingdom. Many people will claim to be Christian, but their true desire is to be served, to be fed, and to consume. Serving these people is hard, expensive work with very little kingdom fruit. In the missionary framework, church leaders strive to serve the 20 percent; it is the apostle who is served, and in turn, the mission itself is expanded. The role of the centralized church is to serve those who serve others and, in so doing, multiply their ministry.

Since every believer is called to do the work of mission, in my view the only justification for taking a salary is to multiply mission work through equipping and empowering others. The mandate to equip others should apply not only to paid leaders, but to all the structures of the church. They should all have a bias to serve and support those who are reaching the lost, serving the poor, and expanding the boundaries of the kingdom. These are the people who should get the full attention and full resources of the centralized church leadership and their systems.

In the prevailing framework, the 20 percent, made up of dedicated non-paid church members, are often distracted from true mission by the demands of volunteering in the centralized ministry, largely serving the nominal and uncommitted "sheep." But in the missionary framework, they are released to engage the lost world in meaningful mission and, even more, they are strengthened and undergirded by the resources and support of the whole group.

Doing the Numbers

Imagine a staff of ten people that run a conventional church. They might marshal another 100 volunteers (the productive minority) to serve the rest of the church. At best, those ten people rally 100 volunteers to serve 1,000 people who have come for a spectacle or to consume some aspect of church life (see Fig. 1). The result is often a self-contained, missionless church framework. The only hope for mission is for nonbelievers to be included in the 1,000 recipients. Indeed, this has been the primary missional fruit of

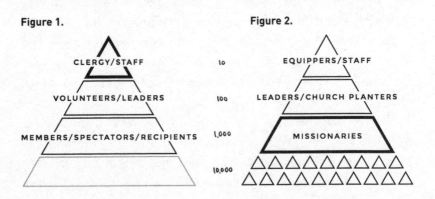

Figure 1.

CLERGY/STAFF — 10

VOLUNTEERS/LEADERS — 100

MEMBERS/SPECTATORS/RECIPIENTS — 1,000

10,000

Figure 2.

EQUIPPERS/STAFF

LEADERS/CHURCH PLANTERS

MISSIONARIES

this model, which puts the priesthood at the top and limits leadership to a very elite group of people.

Consider, as an alternative, the same ten people repurposed as equippers (see Fig. 2). They see their role as serving not the 1,000 potential members, but the 100 potential apostolic leaders. They see their role as mobilizing the productive minority for the work of mission. They do not come with a master plan or take on the role of Jesus in these disciples' lives. Instead, they help those 100 people find the calling and assignment God is already given them, and they help them follow through with it. The result is a group of 100 people that then reach and release 1,000 more people. This is the real priesthood, where the real strength is. The biggest difference is that these people who have been reached do not see themselves merely as sheep, but they understand themselves to be missionaries too because each of those leaders and planters will be expected to do what the first ten did for them—equip and release. They too will want to help others find their calling and serve in a part of this world to which only they have access.

So the people reached and influenced by the 100 then find their way back to the ten who are ready to walk alongside them as they had for that initial 100. In our view, this is the full function of the church. This stands in stark contrast to the prevailing model, which holds us back from this multiplicative effect and unconsciously disempowers the people it reaches by confining them to a limiting structure.

This approach means only ten people need to be paid, with 10,000 reached, instead of ten people maintaining 1,000 people. And while this all started for the UNDERGROUND as a theory (and the numbers are rounded here, for clarity), I can report—at least in our experience—that these estimates are very close to the effect that a missionary framework has had for us. And it is all predicated on the initial decision to serve and equip the 20 percent, to "go with the goers," as they say.

What about the rest?

Of course, I believe the church should serve the needs of the 80 percent and everyday people. In fact, I am convinced that taking care of the sheep is a vital function of the church. What I am describing here is a change of emphasis, not an either/or dichotomy. I mean that we should focus on empowering the 20 percent, without neglecting the 80 percent. However, instead of balancing the two, the church today has largely chosen to call the enterprise of a few paid clergy members "church," which leaves the rest of the body of Christ disengaged and disinterested. Shane Hipps calls the prevailing framework "church as spectacle," and so it is. When the main work of ministry is something that happens from a platform with a crowd watching, is it any wonder we have a church full of spectators? Most churches don't gather a massive crowd, but they want to. The ones who draw the crowds create a kind of frenzy for the best stage performance and the celebrity pastor. But since Jesus was explicit in his prohibition against acts of public worship that build the ego and expand political influence, I suggest this: don't do it.[5]

I am not proposing that the church should neglect the needs of uncommitted people. On the contrary, I am suggesting that real mission work be given to the strength and core of the church, to its most committed people. If Luther was right and we are all called to be priests, then the priestly duty belongs to all of us. The core work of ministry to preach, heal, and confront evil must be done by the people, what is typically called "the laity." We are— all of us—called into that work. Imagine for a moment if every Christian really took this to heart, if all who received Jesus also saw themselves as his ambassadors to the world. Even more, what if every ambassador offered their body as a living sacrifice, burning for God's purposes in the world? Not only would we see an explosion of creative mission reaching every conceivable corner of this country, but we would also see a whole new set of needs emerge for the superstructure of the church to meet, the needs of equipping the sent Christian. And these are precisely the needs that the centralized church should meet. The pathway toward creating the UNDERGROUND was first reimagining church and then imagining the needs that the core people would have. There were no working models that we could find for this.

When everyone is engaged in mission, new needs emerge and even known commodities, like gathering or training, radically change. The normal needs are still there, perhaps even more so, but the nature of, the frequency of, and the content of our gatherings all change. Part of what this new model suggests is that the people of God do the work of God and that, in turn, we create superstructures to serve and nurture the people doing the work. If we collect offerings for shared events and services, we have an obligation to make sure those services and events are *not* something individual, small ecclesial communities could do on their own. The reason is because we want to empower individuals, as well as individual communities, to do what they can do.

The UNDERGROUND decided to focus almost entirely on the 20 percent. In fact, you cannot even really be part of the movement without being engaged in mission. You can attend events, but if you are not involved in mission work, they will not be designed for you. It is not that we deny access to nominal Christians or to the unengaged, it is that our services and programs are not imagined with those populations in mind. When the average American Christian comes to something that does not cater to them, they usually leave, and so it is with us. We do not have to exclude anyone because our approach does the work for us.

Getting a Fresh Start

In Acts 3, a crowd gathers around Peter looking for some answers after he has performed a miracle. He proclaims the gospel and calls for repentance. I have always found the turn of his phrase in this call to be strange: "Repent, then, and turn to God, so that your sins may be wiped out, that times of refreshing may come from the Lord."[6] He makes this beautiful connection between repentance, forgiveness, and a fresh start. This word from Peter is not just a word for new converts, it is a word for the church today. We too must repent for the ways we have not empowered people, for the ways we've underestimated and tried to control the church. We need to repent for the church at large, for all the needs of missional people we have not even attempted to meet. We need those sins to be wiped out. We need a clean slate and a new beginning. We need to be refreshed by the gift of starting over. Maybe repentance is only made more difficult by our sunk cost bias. We have already invested so much into our current church systems that it is painful to even consider repenting about them. But if we want "times of refreshing" to come, repentance may be the only way. In many ways, this whole story is a story of repentance and refreshing.

Since that fresh start in the lives of those in the UNDERGROUND, our commitment to serve these microexpressions of the church and their leaders has made us keenly aware of what apostolic leaders need. While there is so much momentum right now in churches and communities around North America about how to integrate mission into existing churches, all this work has the potential to come to naught without one essential ingredient. As noble as our efforts can be, traditional frameworks will inevitably work against the goal of empowerment. Repentance must come first for meaningful fruit to follow.

Large organizations seem to have an immune system that attacks innovation. Sometimes this process is malicious and premeditated, but most of the time, it's unconscious. It is simply the nature of an existing system to preserve its operating model. This is partly why I felt the need to make a clean break from those systems. It's why we needed to start with no demands other than serving the mission of God. *The result of our experience is not so much what a church that tries to embrace mission can do, but what a group of people who conceive church in an utterly different way— from the vantage point of mission—can do.*

Thus, as we have grown, we have added more and more ways to equip our people. We have increasingly improved ways to give small startups of missional entrepreneurs what they need. Our systems are lean and resist bureaucracy. Everything we do must help our microchurches grow and endure. We have no tradition to uphold, and we ask ourselves every day, *How can we better serve the microchurches?* As our staff has grown from two to twenty, God has helped us build systems and services tailored to our needs. Our purpose is to help our people thrive. That purpose is served by five departments, each operating as a team to provide cutting edge support for anyone engaged in mission. These departments are training, finance, coaching, facilities, and media.

Being a microchurch is the only qualification for getting any of the services we provide. We are built not to serve the needs of the individual, but those of the community on mission. Individuals cannot join the UNDERGROUND; they can join a microchurch, or they can come to get help finding their calling so we can help them form a team and start a microchurch themselves. On the other hand, if a team that is working with kids in foster care, for example, comes to us, then we are ready to receive them. As long as they agree with our Manifesto (our creed), agree to a certain standard of conduct (our covenant), and meet the criteria for being the church (our ecclesial minimum), then the answer is "yes." It's always "yes."

These groups and microchurches have access to everything we have. All we have becomes theirs. We give freely what the prevailing framework has been reluctant to give, namely, permission. Overnight, a small ministry that has come to us for help will have an accounting department to handle their books, donation processing, payroll, expenses, and the like. They will have a media department to help them create videos, websites, a logo, and other print and digital media. They will be assigned a coach to help them navigate their own goals. They will instantly have access to dozens of high-quality ministry training opportunities. They can apply for a portion of the thousands of dollars in grants we give away each year. So far, for all who need and want it, we have been able to provide offices to work from, conference rooms to reserve, and conference facilities for events. Perhaps the best thing of all— these groups gain entry into our beautiful community of leaders. All overnight, and all for free.

This is what we mean by empowerment. First, it is to give permission, and then it is to really get behind the apostolic leader. I have never been comfortable with acceptance of the notion that 20 percent of people in churches do most of the work and mission. To some degree, the UNDERGROUND represents an inversion of the Pareto principle. Virtually all our people are engaged in active mission, with the minority falling somewhere between micro-church involvement or just observing. I am not sure if we have defied the nature of things (something that is certainly possible in the kingdom) or if we have just found a way to nurture the 20 percent who have long been neglected. Either way, the result is very encouraging for those hungry for a church form with greater impact and transformational potential.

Loving the Small

The challenge in this church model is being comfortable with smaller numbers than one might achieve if building for the 80 percent. In Figure 1, there is the possibility of gathering 1,000 people in a room. In Figure 2, there might only be half that number of people in a room. This, too, has been our experience. We can't get over 500 of our people in a room. I sometimes ask church planters when they start out, "If you had to decide today to have either a church of 1,000 people who come together on Sunday but never more than 100 in active mission in the world *or* a church of 1,000 on active mission but never more than 100 in the same room at the same time, which would you choose?" Sadly, even though most of us admit that the latter is better for the kingdom, many still choose the former. Until this changes in the hearts of our leaders, I am sure we will have neither the courage nor the will to make the necessary changes. But if we continue to forge ahead and make the changes, I am also confident that God will give us both the courage and the will.

When all is said and done, I am at peace that the UNDERGROUND's identity has become that of "Christian activists." What can I say? We are a community that lives out what we believe. It is part of the fabric of who we are. While our numbers are smaller than most growing church entities, we have mobilized a network of hundreds of small, autonomous missionary churches and nonprofits. We are a home for the 20 percent dissatisfied with typical churches. Those who want righteousness merely by association or who want to experience church as a spectacle do not last in our community. There have been many days that have made me deeply sad for them and for us, because the truth is that when we fail to live into the fullness of what God has for us, we all miss out.

It is not always easy to deny the masses what they want. We have felt the sting of holding a missionary standard when people who just want a place to worship or learn have fallen in and out of love with us. My heart has fallen for the critical people who know that churches need to change but who, in the end, want someone else to usher in that change. The UNDERGROUND is different because everyone is committed to the change they want to see. We have learned that when each of us lays down our life, the result is that we become the true church. Flaws and failures are still present, but somehow our engagement with God, his mission, and our own ongoing discipleship makes us authentic.

The basic framework of the UNDERGROUND is so different from the prevailing framework of most Western churches because we have focused on the few. Our hope is that, in turn, the few will serve the rest of the world as the hands, feet, and voice of Jesus. Maybe one day God will call all of us to plant microchurches that serve the 20 percent, the most committed. Maybe we will some-day see larger churches that empower and provide resources to the most committed, standing with them in their fidelity to the kingdom of God. If we do, I am convinced we are more likely to see the gospel penetrate all the places where conventional churches cannot go. A church focused on the 20 percent who are goers will no longer ask them to serve the uncommitted Christian, but rather the unbelieving world. After repentance, reimagining how we conceive the church and its function is the first change we have to embrace—but it is far from the last. Wanting to do some-thing and actually doing it are two very different things, but this new framework has given us the freedom to build something new in the empty space between vision and fulfillment.

Chapter 4

FOUNDATIONS

The most abundant, least expensive, most underutilized and constantly abused resource in the world is human ingenuity.

DEE HOCK

In order to understand the foundations of the UNDERGROUND, it helps to think of it as a network of autonomous members, not a monolithic institution. This structure, in part, comes down to control. Networks exhibit less control over their constituents, while institutions maintain higher control over their parts. The structure of the UNDERGROUND reflects our belief that we are speeding toward a time when communities of people will be understood through the lens of network instead of through the traditional views of institutions. We are also quickly approaching the twilight of mechanisms like command and control leadership, narrow and restrictive vision statements, and homogeneous communities.

We became convinced that in order to build a new kind of church in a networked world, we would have to understand networks and how to employ them for the formation of the church. In other words, the number of people you can fit in your building should no longer be a primary metric for a vibrant, verdant, and missional community. Instead, we should be measuring things like the creativity and diversity of the networks we are forming. We consider ourselves to be a network of networks. Each of our communities is considered a microchurch (read micronetwork) and as a whole, those networks are connected together as a macronetwork.

I am convinced that these kinds of contextualized and diversified church networks will soon take the place of the local church, as we know it. Until this happens, the ones who are willing to lead at the forefront of this shift will stand apart as new wine in new wineskins. The change from institution to network will take at least four foundational shifts in the cognitive and practical life of the new community. A new kind of indispensable church built on these foundations will win the eyes of the cities where they grow.

These four ideas have served as the foundation for everything we've built and have created a missionary community:

- Size—the size of the thing we call church
- Calling—the way churches are born
- Servanthood—the nature of church leadership
- Abundance—the mindset that allows churches to grow, thrive, and usher in the kingdom

Foundation 1: Size

The church, in its most potent form, is small.

Bigger is not necessarily better. If I think about the best restaurants in my city, I don't even consider seating capacity. Instead, what makes something like a restaurant a civic treasure or indispensable to the life and culture of a city is more about its quality and uniqueness, it's not really about how big it is. More than that, the restaurant has to somehow embody the heart of the city. Every city has restaurants like this—places with reputations that precede them, where people say, "Oh, if you are ever in Tampa, you have to eat there."

For too long people in church leadership have imagined the size of their church to be a measure of its significance or success. Pastors size each other up based on weekend attendance. What I propose is that churches imagine a new measurement, something more like an iconic city restaurant known by its quality, not its size. What if every Christian who visited your city heard, "Oh, if you are ever in Cleveland, you have to visit _____ church"? What if churches—not their leaders—were so unique and indispensable to their cities that you just had to check them out? Again, I don't think a large seating capacity holds much novelty anymore. In fact, it may do harm to the next generation of kingdom seekers. It is not the size of the church that makes it valuable. It is something else, something deeper and more lasting.

One of the great revivals in terms of numerical growth in church history has taken place in China over the last 100 years. It has happened, at least in part, because the church units there have been reconfigured as something very small. In 1982, there were reportedly 1.3 million Christians in China, and within twenty years, that number had risen to 90 million.[1] Scholars predict that by 2025 China will be the most populous Christian nation in the world.[2] Millions of Chinese individuals have heard and responded to the good news about Jesus, forming hundreds of thousands of underground house churches and small groups devoted to disciple-making. Studying this phenomenon is both inspiring and frustrating, as we are faced with the cold reality that the same God and the same gospel we offer the Western world is simply not producing the same results.

Researchers like David Garrison have attempted to bottle the lightning of Chinese church practices by reducing them to certain principles. Still, our attempt to embody every one of these principles leaves us counting growth by the dozens, not the thousands. I believe some of this comes down to structure since we still largely refuse to fully embrace a mission model of empowerment.

One missionary to China told me that 60 percent of all Chinese house churches are led by teenage girls. I have no way of confirming that, but the idea is so jarring that response alone proves the point. This kind of wholesale empowerment is unheard of in the Western church. Still, this kind of growth begs for a response from our weaker, seemingly less effective models.

Some of the growth of the Chinese church is fueled by solidarity with those suffering hardship in service to the church—through repression, harassment, and detention. It is counterintuitive but true, nevertheless, that the church thrives (in the ways that matter most) when it is under duress. Throughout history, the underground church did not really suffer imposters, because persecution has a way of filtering the poseurs from the pack, leaving only the truly converted and the totally committed. That kind of potency is also a matter for reflection: When we plant churches by sending out flyers, what type of people do we expect to draw in? When missional outreach is primarily through mail-outs, what type of calling do we expect recipients to hear?

If we can take away only one revelation from the work of God in the Chinese church, it should be that enormous growth can happen by honoring a small, simple, and minimalist version of the church. Trying to replicate the growth of the Chinese church in the West is a fool's errand, because there are simply too many differences between our cultures in context and milieu. What we can see (and admire), however, is a church that is, in fact, uniquely Chinese. It is not an import from another place, and it is not trying to hold on to some historical expression that does not respect the forces and factors at work in the lives of the people who find hope and a home in their churches. Perhaps the best thing that happened to the Chinese church was for the Western missionaries to be expelled. The result is not just a growing church, but a contextualized one. I don't mean to enshrine the Chinese church or build it up to mythological proportions; I merely intend to honor an expression of church that is a product of its time, place, and people—its context. It is vital, adaptive, and growing. That's what I want for the North American church and beyond.

During our time living and working in Asia, we came to the two-fold conclusion that, on the one hand, we have a lot to learn from the church in the East and, on the other hand, those lessons simply would not play out the same way in a Western context. We had to do our own work of contextualization. We knew that what we were seeing and experiencing would have to be *adapted*, and not simply *adopted*, if we wanted to see the same kind of fruit. The cultural distinction is too important to ignore.

In the spirit of contextualization, during the early days of the UNDERGROUND, we were conceiving a church guided more by our values (as expressed in our Manifesto; see Appendix A) than by a particular ministry paradigm or mission statement. While we knew that a clearly expressed mission would be helpful and effective, we also believed our mission, as we understood it, was as broad as the Great Commission and that our methodology needed to remain flexible and adjust to the changing world we hoped to reach. Our values have remained constant, offering us clear and consistent guidance as we work out the *how* of our mission. We stand by our values, all the while knowing they are not unique to us. These are values that have been held by the church throughout the centuries. Yet, we also know that our steadfast adherence to them—and the prioritization of mission over other biblical values—will (we hope) be a prophetic call to the church in our context.

Our Ecclesial Minimum

I want to outline some practical applications of our "ecclesial minimum" here.[3] We knew that the UNDERGROUND's ecclesiology had to be simple because we wanted to value the microchurch as the most basic expression of the church. By making a small size part of our definition of church, we opened up the possibility for more churches—and more contextualized churches—to form. We concluded that when Christians work together in sincere worship and genuine community to accomplish a part of the mission of God, they function as the church. Worship, community, and mission, then, are the ecclesial minimum. This means that church *can include more elements*, but not less. We encourage biblically appointed leadership, sacramental worship, the pursuit of the gifts of the Spirit, and giving, but while these are desired components, they are not required for a group to be a microchurch. We believe these churches also need the larger network, leadership, and resources of a citywide church to strengthen, empower, and help direct their expression. We gather for worship, training, and leadership, primarily to strengthen and supply the microchurches in their labor to obey Jesus and proclaim the good news of the kingdom in their mission field. We

WORSHIP

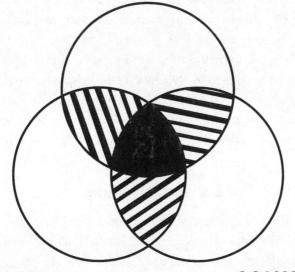

MISSION   **COMMUNITY**

believe the larger church expression exists to serve the smaller, not the other way around.

The church in all its simplicity and beauty is the thing we wanted to see reproduced, but we also suspected that the language of reproduction was only really appealing to the people at the top of the pyramid. When leaders get excited about reproduction or multiplication, it can become a new form of empire-building or personal ambition. We wanted to abandon the futile competition for the biggest church, with one pastor as the celebrity, which measures value and impact by the number of people in attendance. But how would we keep from making the size of one's network the new scale for competitive envy?

We ran into a challenge, because even thinking about what *top leaders* need or what *top leaders* are motivated by is to miss the point. We had to start thinking about what moves and motivates *the rank and file believer* to act like a disciple-maker or a church planter—not just about what motivates *top leaders*. Now we think about the ethic of sacrificial love Jesus engendered among his followers. Jesus gave his disciples a massive mission, but he broke it down into something each of them could do. Disciple-making is a gift to us because it puts the work of transformation on the level of life-on-life experience, thus democratizing it in a way that includes everyone. More than that, the great promise of faithfulness to that mission is not the subduing of the world (which would only appeal to the vainglorious), but it is instead the promise of his presence. If we do not abandon him, he will be with us "to the very end of the age."[4]

While reproduction and multiplication are a part of God's design for the growth of his church and the coming of his kingdom, they should be our primary motivation. At least in the Western context, we need another lens through which we see the church reproducing. We need empowered expressions of the church small enough for every devoted disciple to lead, and each one as different as the people leading them.

Foundation 2: Calling

Everyone has a missionary calling.

We have come to discover that our emphasis on calling is something that almost every Christian appreciates, but few churches share. It is a strange irony that a church model built on giving consumers what they want has so badly missed the felt need of so many people. The truth is that people want to know their calling and to live in it. But this requires attention, discernment, and guidance. You have to wonder, then, why there is such a conspicuous absence of church programs to help people discover it. Whether conscious or not, I have come to believe that church leaders know they cannot go down that rabbit hole because of what it would produce. To allow people access to this kind of power—the voice of God—is to unleash an almost uncontrollable force. It is to risk everyone no longer having the time, energy, or interest to serve established church programs. Their time and, perhaps most disconcerting of all, their money, will be more and more engaged outside the walls of the church building. This is, of course, exactly what we at the UNDERGROUND hope for.

Once people who feel called by God to serve and see the kingdom go outside the church walls, church leaders often feel like they *lose them*, in a very real sense, for the internal workings of a labor-intensive centralized church. So perhaps churches and their leaders have not helped people discover their calling because these leaders sense it will be the end of the world as they know it. Nevertheless, the ability to hear and follow one's calling is something people crave and on which the future of the church depends.

Reviving Calling

What is "calling" after all? And why do people crave it? It is the intersection of two things: intimacy and mission. On the one hand, we want to hear God speak to us personally, which represents a very intimate connotation of calling. When God calls me, he uses my name. Consider the implications of that: it means he knows me and wants me. When I call for one of my kids, I expect them to come. Occasionally, the one who hears me shouting is not the one who is being called. But even then, that child feels an obligation to relay the message, which is the same, "Dad wants you." This is the first and most beautiful implication of calling. The Father wants you.

God calls you because he loves, knows, and has something for just you. It astonishes the mind and fills the heart. This is why people need to know they are being called—because mission must begin with that moment of being known and loved by God. Even Jesus, who was secure and sufficient in a way we cannot comprehend, apparently needed this kind of calling. At his baptism in the Jordan River, he heard the voice of his Father affirm him, "You are my beloved son." This calling took place before any mission was embarked upon.

We want and need God to speak to us personally, but likewise, we want to know the purpose to which we are called. This is the second type of calling. While it's still personal, it goes beyond affirmation into mission. We all carry a suspicion that we are made for something—that life is not without meaning and that the creator God has made each of us in his own image to create and build like he does. We know (or at least we hope) that there is some task to which we alone are called. We long for something that will give us eternal purpose and satisfaction. This sense of calling is the way the term is used even in secular parlance. To find one's calling, they say, is to find the thing you are uniquely good at, work that comes easy or gives us a great sense of significance and fulfillment. This connotation of calling speaks to finding our unique place in the mission of God. God is calling forth his kingdom, and we are not just meant to pray his kingdom come, but to live toward that end. Each one of us has a job in ushering in that kingdom and speeding the day of its coming, and there is nothing in this world that will give us the same joy, sustenance, or satisfaction than living in that calling. It is what Jesus called his "food"—to do the will of the Father who sent him.[5]

The degree to which we have ignored our calling is the degree to which we have degraded our individual and collective lives, preventing the full expansion of God's kingdom. Calling is the fulfillment of our craving for both intimacy and mission. It is personal, and it is social; it is a journey inward and outward; calling is where God's love for me and God's love for others overlaps. You want to know how to get people close to Jesus? Help them hear his voice calling them. You want to know how to get people on mission? Same.

The UNDERGROUND experiment has been predicated on the idea that everyone is both *called* and *capable* of discerning that call.[6] The result is a diversity of missional church expressions that are creative and innovative beyond the imagination of any single leader. We have discovered that when people listen to their calling, niche ministries emerge, reaching into gaps we didn't even know were there. The result is a missionary engagement that far exceeds anything a megaministry could execute. Consider what is gained through this approach: the leaders are almost always indigenous. The ministry ideas are creative and in many cases utterly original. The approach affords at least the possibility of total penetration because the God who sees all things, inhabits all places, and loves all people without prejudice or ignorance is the one doing the sending. No strategy will reach every kind of person except a strategy that mobilizes every kind of person.

Foundation 3: Servanthood

Only servants should lead.

I mentioned in the introduction the idea that we are now operating in a creative economy. More than ever, commerce trades what is created, not what is manufactured. The difference is subtle but meaningful, especially when we think about how the church might grow over the next decade and beyond. People need to be allowed creative control over the expression of church in which they serve. The mass production of one rigid model is not appealing to the next generation of leaders the church needs to cultivate.

Creative Control

This discussion of the forms of church expression includes calling, as well. Once we have settled on the ecclesial minimum (all churches must express the three heuristics of community, mission, and worship somehow)—the *what*—of church, the rest—the *how*—is left to the localized leader to dream, create, and contextualize. This is the next level of empowerment because it is not just giving people permission to lead, it is also giving them creative control over what they lead. The church has to be simplified into something that can express itself in very different ways and in very different contexts, partly because it will affect those contexts, but also because leaders need this ability to shape their particular mission in order to say yes. They have to believe they are a part of creating something that is both unique and important in the world. Creating an expression of the church gives an order of magnitude to what might otherwise be a simple idea. But being allowed autonomy over that idea and how it is implemented gives leaders passion and ownership, which is powerful and self-sustaining.

Asking people to hear and respond to their own passion and unique calling captures both the dynamics of movements (i.e., "multiplication potential") and the Western need for creative autonomy. The value for us at the UNDERGROUND is expressed as empowerment, but there is no kingdom empowerment without calling. We want to empower people, yes, but not indiscriminately. We want to empower people to do what God has called them to do. I think of it as empowered obedience, which primarily takes the form of servanthood.

Empowered Servants

Just like the original work of the church, which started at Pentecost, our obedience is only made possible by the work of the Holy Spirit. Nothing should be planted or initiated that is not inspired and confirmed by the voice and will of God. I cannot really give someone permission to start a church or ministry. Ultimately, that authority must come from the leadership of God through his Spirit. Still, empowerment and permission-giving is an important part of what we do. But empowerment, in practical terms, is not about giving people the right *to do something*, it is about connecting them to the authority *they already have* from God. The result is that they can do the thing God wants them to do. A big part of what we do is to simply say "yes." Many people have ideas of what God might want them to do, something God has embedded into their hearts or heads that they would like to see changed, but they have just not been encouraged or equipped to do it.

Christian empowerment means helping people hear the voice of God on a personal level. It is more about leading people into the genesis of their own Pentecost than it is about laying out some visionary master plan that moves them to action. In a very real sense, forms of leadership that instruct rather than empower are a threat to Spirit-empowered missionary engagement. If people are moved merely by my eloquence or my vision for the future, for example, they become dependent on me as the engineer and keeper of that vision. If, on the other hand, their own vision for life and the kingdom comes through an encounter with God, then they are conversely dependent on him for the renewal and vitality of that vision, leaving me as an encourager, not the originator. The release of this burden is vital for effective, long-term missional engagement of network leaders.

We play a dangerous game when we elevate superstructure leaders to the place of the primary visionary. I understand the heart behind these actions and sentiments, but the peril is in the potential to elevate the leader, instead of humbling the leader. God is and always will be the visionary. Our role as leaders is to make space for people to hear God—nothing more, nothing less.

Consider Paul's breathtakingly radical depiction of this kind of leadership: "For what we preach is not ourselves, but Jesus Christ as Lord, and ourselves as your servants for Jesus' sake."[7] Jesus is Lord. The leaders are not. This hierarchy must be supported not only by our sermons and the practice of our lives, but also by the structures we endorse and the influence we exert.

We decided to build the UNDERGROUND on a leadership model that insists on what Robert Greenleaf called "servant-leader." Greenleaf prophesied fifty years ago, in his groundbreaking book *Servant Leadership*, that the future would demand servants who learn to lead, not leaders who learn to serve. The distinction is important. Written in the turmoil of the 1960s, and perhaps ahead of his time, Greenleaf predicted that next generation followers "will not casually accept the authority of existing institutions. Rather, they will freely respond only to individuals who are chosen as leaders because they are proven and trusted as servants."[8] This is not a novel concept, just an aptly spoken term. Jesus himself describes these types of leaders throughout his ministry. Jesus's vision for his followers was that they would become a new kind of leader, servant-leaders.

You know that rulers of the Gentiles lord it over them, and their high officials exercise authority over them. Not so with you. Instead, whoever wants to become great among you must be your servant, and whoever wants to be first must be your slave—just as the Son of Man did not come to be served, but to serve, and to give his life as a ransom for many.[9]

This conviction makes leadership accessible to every mature disciple, not just the talented few. Perhaps we see so little engagement in the American church because we have not offered Christians an entry that is accessible to them. If what it means to be a preacher or a Christian leader is to stand on a stage with a microphone, then have we not needlessly reduced the pool of people who can lead to the number of people who have a good stage presence? Not only is this mentality anathema to the gospel Jesus preached, it is strategically foolish for a movement that wants to grow. Reviving the concept of servanthood, therefore, as the primary quality of Christian leadership is necessary for the kind of movement we imagine. Empowerment means helping people to hear their calling and to understand themselves as servants to a group of people who are lost or poor and in need of the kingdom.

At the place of ascension, Jesus told his shell-shocked followers to go to Jerusalem and wait. And he told them what they were waiting for—the Holy Spirit to fall and empower. This must remain the first hope and patient pursuit of all who would be a part of the kingdom. Wait to be empowered. What then is the work of church community servants and leaders if not to serve the Word and wish of God as revealed in the place of the Spirit's empowering? This is the reordering we have considered and to which we have submitted. This is not just a theological conviction, it is also a cultural revelation. That is to say, this is not just something the Bible mandates, it is something the people of God crave.

Foundation 4: Abundance

There is more than enough.

The last foundation of the UNDERGROUND is the notion of abundance. Take an example of abundance from an important and insightful book, *Exponential Organizations*, where Salim Ismail tells the story of Finnish mobile phone company Nokia and their $8.1 billion acquisition of Navteq, a mapping and navigation company that was built around in-road sensor technology. Navteq commanded such a high price because they had cornered the market on the expensive sensors that had to be installed in roads all over the world in order to monitor and report traffic flow. It was an acquisition predicated on scarcity that said, "These are the only sensors, and if we want into this market, we have to buy them."

Around the same time, a small Israeli company called Waze was born. Ismail explains,

> Instead of making a massive capital investment in in-road sensor hardware, the founders of Waze chose instead to crowdsource location information by leveraging the GPS sensors on its users phones . . . to capture traffic information. Within two years Waze was gathering traffic data from as many sources as Navteq had road sensors, and within ten years it had ten times as many sources. What's more, the cost of adding each new source was essentially zero, not to mention that Waze's users regularly upgrade their phones—and thus Waze's information base. In contrast the Navteq system cost a fortune to upgrade.[10]

The story of Waze is a routine narrative in the creator economy, and it represents the potential of an abundance mindset and the results of operating from its suppositions. In 2013, Waze was acquired by Google for $1.1 billion, even though it had less than 100 employees and no hardware. I like to imagine what 100 people could do with the message of the kingdom, if only they had the abundance mindset Jesus asked us to have.

Consider other companies, like Waze, who know abundance. Airbnb is now one of the largest providers of lodging in America, and they don't own a single bed. Uber is quickly replacing the taxi industry, and they don't own a single car. Wikipedia is the most comprehensive encyclopedia in the world, but it has never paid for a single article. Crowdsourcing, crowdfunding, and flash mobs all represent the abundance of this new world we inhabit.

Opening Our Eyes

The story of the woman at the well occurs only in John's Gospel. Concerned mostly with the metanarrative of cosmology and theology, John reveals the divinity of Jesus even as he walked among ordinary people like this woman. He tells this story of Jesus's almost scandalous interaction with a Samaritan woman and follows it with some of Jesus's words about the harvest. The message is about abundance and our ability to see (or to not see) what is really there. By the end of this story, the whole town of Samaritans comes out to see Jesus, full of faith because of the woman's testimony about him. In this moment, Jesus says to them: "I tell you, open your eyes and look at the fields! They are ripe for harvest."[11] He knew the abundance of the harvest fields, and he was sharing his awareness with his disciples.

Abundance is a mindset as much as it is a reality. We have to see the world differently in order to understand how Jesus changes it. There is potential in us as called people and, in turn, in our networks and communities of churches, if we surrender to the way Jesus sees us. The productive paranoia of the industrial complex must give way to the hopeful enterprise of this new and networked world. Hierarchies reinforce scarcity, and networks will soon devour hierarchies. We need the new wine for the new wineskin.

Nowhere is this truer than in the church. If we think about disciple-making or church planting in the same ways we always have, raising loads of money and building huge physical structures, we will fail to see the abundance of resources at our fingertips—*for free*. People are the great resources of the church, because God has put his Spirit inside his people. Therefore, the delivery system for his grace and his message is not a building, but is instead this "treasure in jars of clay."[12] He is building us into a temple, living stones one upon the other. This conception of the church is not a novelty; it is both ancient and new. It is a foundational idea for something like the UNDERGROUND. We have had to reimagine how we see the world. There is abundance and possibly out there, and in how we see ourselves, as well. We are called and are equipped with every good thing we need.

Change starts with realizing that the strength and significance of a church is not the building it owns, the grounds it keeps, or the advertising budget it maintains. It is not the size of its stage or the magnitude of its children's ministry. The church is its people. There are megaministries that seat thousands but have less cultural impact on the neighborhoods in which they host events than a church composed of 100 individuals who are all called and empowered to bring the kingdom into their neighborhoods.

Cultural transformation is almost impossible to measure, so it is hard to know exactly what the result of this kind of realignment could really be. But it is not hard to imagine that smaller, empowered mission work is faster, more customized, and even more fulfilling to the people doing it. Deep down, we have to believe that when the church is functioning in all its fullness, it will be able to accomplish both.

The UNDERGROUND shows proof that when this mindset of

abundance is laid as the foundation of a community, missionary potential is unlocked. Keep in mind, though, that each micro-church has its own metrics for what it considers success. Our work is not to control the church, but to let it go—to allow it to fill every crack and crevice in our city, to have the courage to see the depth of depravity and need in our cities, and in turn, to have the courage to see the resources and power of the people of God available to all.

It is hard to put into words the strange feeling of both excitement and trepidation we felt in the early days of forming the UNDERGROUND, when we were taking on a seemingly Herculean task. I was not convinced the principles behind our four foundations would all work, but I was sure they were the right cornerstones from which to build. The beginning of a thing is always a matter of principle. Still, we have been at this long enough now to be able to move confidently beyond theory and principle. And we are ready to share some of the results of our sustained commitment to these foundational ideas in order that it might motivate other, like-minded individuals, churches, and groups who are out there living life in the kingdom.

RESULTS

*The first Velvet Underground album only sold 10,000
copies, but everyone who bought it formed a band.*

BRIAN ENO

Before we address the question of effectiveness, it should be said that, on one very important level, I don't think it should matter. Don't get me wrong—I am as pragmatic as anyone when it comes to ideas, and I love to create an environment where risk and experimentation are rewarded. We never really know if a theory will work, so we try the idea out and celebrate whatever we learn, whether we "win" or "lose." Still, there are deeper motivations that require commitment, just because they are right and because they are an expression of the kingdom of God. Sometimes new ideas will not work because they aren't meant to "work."

The ministry of John the Baptist, that voice crying in the wilderness, was a faithful one. He was not a pragmatist; he was a prophet. Crowds of people came to him precisely because he pulled no punches. The prophet's voice is sometimes heeded and sometimes not, but regardless of the effect, the prophet must cry out. For that reason, John had to internalize a different measurement of success. He could not have known it or liked it, but for him, ultimately success was to die. I think it is important for all serious disciples, all planters, all activists, and all leaders to ask themselves if they will simply be who God is calling them to be, even if their mission work doesn't "succeed" in a conventional sense.

Does It Work?

The individuals who made up the original UNDERGROUND team experienced so much frustration working in churches we did not build and laboring in structures we did not design or even fully understand. One very real goal for me was to start something that, as best I understood, was a faithful representation of the church in the world. If none but those first few dozen of us ever noticed our work and if our ideas never caught on, I wondered, would I stay faithful to it? That's a question we all have to ask ourselves in our own situation. These deeper convictions have to do with identity, and they have to do with obedience. I had to face my own demons of success, performance, and numeric affirmation *before* I started the UNDERGROUND, otherwise they would have gotten in the way. I had to wrestle with my own heart until I was truly persuaded. Before considering metrics of any kind, I think all aspiring movement leaders should do the same in their own hearts.

Multiplying Microchurches

Having said that, the results of our work should be measured, and each metric, when considered from the position of faithfulness, can motivate and hold us responsible. That is, we *should* count things. However, if we want to change the church as it currently functions, we have to change what we measure. As long as we keep measuring ourselves with the metrics of weekend attendance and offerings, we will not be encouraged to pursue deployment or more decentralized expressions of mission and ministry.

We have to live with deep conviction so we remain faithful even in the absence of visible success. Jesus wanted his disciples to understand that there was a place where treasure was stored that was invisible to the naked eye. It's called the kingdom of God. Still, he gave us outcomes toward which we can hope, pray, and work. He talked of a food we didn't eat, as I mentioned above, which was to do the will of the Father who sends us. That produced a harvest beyond the sight of the naked eye. Jesus insisted that his disciples enter a town with the intention of leaving if no one was receptive to the message of the kingdom. He wanted them to consider effectiveness.

The metric the UNDERGROUND cares most about is the number of microchurches formed. That number stands for calling heard and obeyed, community formed around mission, and (at least in theory) previously unreachable people encountering the gospel and the coming of the kingdom of God. More microchurches means disciples are being made. And this growth does not come through our master planning or expert strategy, but by releasing the people of God to handle the graces (or sacraments) of the church, taking them into the world and offering them to the lost and the poor. As I have already explained, the microchurch concept is entirely predicated on the idea of calling. For us, microchurches are not franchises (like discipleship groups, house churches, or even scaled parachurch ministries); they are customized and contextualized expressions of the church as unique as the people who start them. They hold no particular brand identity with another church.

The more microchurches we help start, the more people we are helping to live their call to obey Jesus, and the more people we are reaching through that obedience. This is the primary measurement of success for us. We work to see that each of these communities thrive and persevere, but as with all start-up ventures, we know that some won't survive, let alone thrive. So, in addition to counting the total number of microchurches in our network, we also want to count the number that we have helped to start, including those that don't continue. We know that not all our ideas will work just right, and keeping track of the microchurches that fail to flourish is important too.

In Luke 10, Jesus sends his followers out in teams of two with the undeniable possibility of mission failure. This potential of "failure" is evident in the instructions he gives them as they depart: "But when you enter a town and are not welcomed . . ." He gives the disciples instructions that not only absolve them from the guilt of failure, but that reinforce the inevitability of failure. He empowers them with the profound truth that to obey him means to go and offer peace; the results of their work, though, are up to God and the people who hear. We have to be careful about equating numeric success (responsiveness) with mission success. The disciples who walk away, shaking the dust from their feet, are equally faithful to the mission of Jesus, because Jesus predicted that kind of nonresponsiveness. He prepared them for this inevitable reality. Of course, this outcome is still cause for grief, not celebration, but even still, it is no less an example of faithful mission.

When a disciple experiences failure, they may pivot their mission location or population, but they do not leave the call of the mission itself. We have found that microchurch failure does not cause people to quit, only to try something else. This is part of the culture of experimentation and what we think is a healthy expression of faithfulness. (I will say more about this in the chapter on surprises.) While counting the number of microchurches active in our network is important, perhaps the more important metric is the number of microchurches we have helped to start. So, both the "incubator component" (number started) and the "support structures" (number that continue) are vital to us.

Despite the difficulty of our stated mission and our fresh approach, we have seen both numbers consistently grow. Apostolic work is hard, particularly when working with marginalized populations. It's important for us to remember that our growth is not always going to translate to more donors or even more leaders. When you work with the mentally ill, for example, or people with disabilities, the homeless, the dying, or the incarcerated—all people of certain mission fields in their own right—you cannot expect the same kind of financial and human capital return on investment that has built the middle-class megachurches. But the work done in and by these communities is nothing less than the kingdom coming and Jesus made flesh.

Understanding why counting individuals is not our primary metric is important, and it reveals why having the right metrics matter. If we count total people involved in microchurches (or who might come to a worship service), then we are predisposed to *not* do ministry in a nearby prison, for example, even though Jesus himself sacralized this ministry, saying it was a ministry to himself.[1] Metrics matter, and how we measure our effectiveness will determine where we invest more time, resources, and energy. Aren't prisoners important to the heart of God? Do not the sick and the troubled hold eternal value to the heart of God, even though they will not commute to our services and sit quietly in their seats, contributing 10 percent of their sizeable incomes? We have to embrace those realities in our hearts in order to faithfully engage these types of mission fields.

The kingdom grows by announcing good news to the poor and to those with small incomes, small attention spans, and small resumes. I am not saying middle-class people are not important to God, only that we have to find a new way of doing church that does not prioritize them above the needy or, even worse, exclude the marginalized precisely because they are weak. That kind of exclusion is not just a mistake; it is a travesty.

We have to find a way to count what matters to the heart of God, a way that is faithful to the enterprise of the church going into the world to seek and save that which was lost. We have to be able to answer any question of our validity with the same answer Jesus gives John, "Go back and report to John what you have seen and heard: The blind receive sight, the lame walk, those who have leprosy are cleansed, the deaf hear, the dead are raised, and the good news is proclaimed to the poor."[2]

It is important to note that our growth is not built solely on the middle class. And releasing our metrics from the tyranny of attendance at a Sunday service has allowed us to reach whole new populations with pride and joy. This makes our growth stand out. We are happy to empower and serve people with a middle-class calling; however, a majority—about 60 percent—of our microchurches have historically focused on a poor or marginalized population.

Multiplying Innovations

More than just counting microchurches, I would say that we want to measure innovation itself. While this is an elusive metric, we want to be able to see that our people are trying, that they are stepping out in faith to be disciples who obey the commission to preach the kingdom and make more disciples. The only way I know to measure something like innovation is to measure the experimental communities deployed. (Innovation is not just a new idea, but a new idea put into action. That's why we measure communities deployed, not just imagined.) This is also why we not only count the number of microchurch ideas we empower and launch, but also the number of leaders who start something new. We want to create an environment where risk and adventure are rewarded. We remain cognizant that counting microchurches alone could also go wrong and descend into a strategy to deploy leaders who will manufacture the minimum viable product as quickly as possible.

When we talk about counting microchurches, we mean innovations of church expressions catalyzed by each leader's personal calling. Each microchurch, then, is an expression of personal commitment and ecclesial innovation. Yet, the work they do is not necessarily new. It could be a house church or a feeding ministry; it could be residential; or it could be decentralized. What is new is the authority given to all to start something and to see themselves as ordained to create and carry out the work of mission. This releasing of the priesthood of all believers represents a massive innovative step forward for the church.

Innovation does not imply disdain for the church in history or even right now. Innovation is only possible when what is strong and good in existing systems is exploited. In other words, much of what the church does (even in the West) is powerful and transcendent. But some of it is not. We are not actually recreating the church. In part, we are returning to the best practices of the church throughout time. That movement looks and feels like innovation, but more often than not, it is actually applying what the church has always meant to do in a new context, with new language and new structures that are informed by the time and place in which the church finds itself. There must be honor for the church's past innovations, even if they no longer make sense.

The UNDERGROUND is not a cell strategy, where we quickly reproduce the same thing or mobilize all our leaders in the same ministry. Our microchurches are unique expressions of the church that are as different as the people who start them. For that reason, each of them represents a new entity—breaking into new space with mission—as well as the formation of a new disciple (at the very least) in the form of the person who leads. Starting and leading churches is what disciples do, and they are formed in doing so. We want people to start unique microchurches because it ushers in the kingdom, not only in the world, but increasingly in them too. You see, microchurches are how we make disciples, in part because that is the core work of the microchurch and in part because we think that nothing forms a person spiritually like taking the step to start and sustain a church. The best discipleship comes through trying to plant, lead, and grow the church. That is kingdom expansion at its finest, God taking more and more ground, even in our own lives.

ACTIVATING INNOVATORS

In his book *Diffusion of Innovation,* Everett Rogers argues that any new idea must be communicated and transmitted first from a small number of people before it is broadly adopted. This diffusion of a new idea or technology requires both time and communication. It is essentially an interactive process. The initial group, who are the innovators, only really influence the next group in line, the early adopters. These early adopters, in turn, influence the early majority, and so on until a larger portion of society, hopefully, adopts the new model. Yet, what strikes me about this model, as I reflect on our journey, is just how small the innovator class is.

According to Rogers, only 2.5 percent of the population is considered innovators. That is to say, less than 3 percent of people

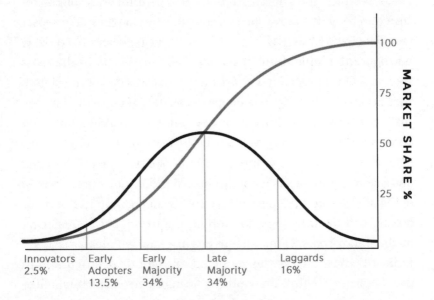

adopt an idea simply because it is a good idea. The vast majority of people need predecessors, a group of people who have already implemented the idea before them. When I think about offering a working alternative to something as entrenched and beloved as the church, that number may be even smaller. If Rogers is right, then it is the innovators and the next group, which he calls early adopters (13.5 percent), that make up the target of our work.

In practical terms, that means our enterprise is left with only 16 percent of the Christian world even willing to consider what we were doing. Add to that the high call for sacrifice, simplicity, and emphasis on the poor, and we face a real challenge to grow. The UNDERGROUND was never going to be a megaministry, as such. However, our focus on the people we're reaching—the poor, the marginalized—means any growth we have experienced has happened despite working against the current of other church growth phenomena. We are contradicting almost all the lessons learned from fast-growing churches and communities in America over the last thirty years and are doing so intentionally.

Still, we want to grow, mostly because we want to see people empowered. But no matter the motivation, an idea is being tested here that will only really be confirmed if people try it. Like it or not, growth and adoption of an idea validate its practice. After all, we are making assumptions about people's hearts in what we do. Part of what we argue is that people want to *do* something—that people have latent and buried passions to lead, love, and serve. We are convinced that calling is something most people are either explicitly aware of or implicitly desire. In the early days, we needed to test these ideas, to see if they were true.

We also needed to resist the marketer's approach to church: branding, packaging, and selling our wares on billboards and mailers. This behavior is distasteful to me personally, and I find it difficult to reconcile this approach with the life and teaching of Jesus. Still, I can see the value in using culturally available mediums for communicating both the gospel and the vision or message of a mission. But for us, for the first ten years at least, we held a conviction to be shy and not to advertise or publicize our idea. We wanted to grow in more organic ways. If, for instance, we resisted potent modern growth mechanisms and instead relied on the more mysterious and quiet form of growth by relationship, we could in turn offer a deeper validation of our core ideas. In other words, with the deck stacked against our growth, if we grew anyway, wouldn't that offer irrefutable proof that we were on to something?

I think so. This was always a major part of the experiment, and it's working. Do people really want to lead, create, and start things? If that isn't true, then the enterprise is doomed. And if it isn't true, then we wanted to find out sooner than later. That's the nature of experimentation, and it's the premise on which all our work is built. If Christians actually want to just attend things and be told what to think and how to live, then our work would find no purchase in the soil of American Christianity.

HAVING SPIRITUAL CHILDREN

We discovered early on that the UNDERGROUND would grow in two ways. To borrow from the language of reproduction, we knew we would have both "natural" children and that we would adopt. With regard to reproduction, some microchurches would be planted from the disciple-making work of existing microchurches. These groups, in theory, would carry the same movement DNA from which they started and would naturally understand our culture and values. With regard to adoption, on the other hand, some microchurches would be metaphorical orphans in the city, serving the poor or working in some area that was unsupported or unsanctioned by the institutional churches from which they came. These unaffiliated missionaries would find in us a home for their hearts and resources for their work.

In the first five years, most of our growth came from natural births—people within existing microchurches who were inspired by the UNDERGROUND culture and community. They were able to finally pursue something that God had put on their hearts. In the next five years, most of our growth came through adoptions. Through the simple passage of time, our reputation in Tampa has grown and our work has become more open and less of a secret. Still, our posture toward growth has always been to simply respond to the needs and the initiation of people asking for help. This, too, has been significant. We have recruited, but there's been no need to recruit.

Consider the very stable growth curve of our work in Tampa: we have grown about 20 percent each year. Our attrition rate (not all groups make it) is about 10 percent per year, which means our planting rate is 30–40 percent per year. So even with that relatively small attrition rate and no attempt to recruit, virtually no publicity, and only the values of service to those with a mission idea, we continue to grow at a significant rate.

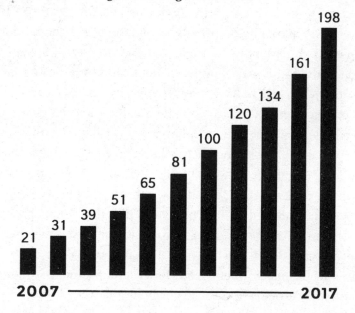

This figure shows what our microchurch growth has looked like in Tampa.

Of course, these are communities, so it is difficult to translate this into number of people reached.[3] Some of these microchurches work with hundreds of individuals; others work with less than twelve. Since the metric that matters to us is empowered communities, counting individuals is not as important in our reports. We want every kind of person to live and be the church where they are, reaching who they feel called to reach in a way that is led by God and tailored to their context. We do not try to control what they do or how effective they are. The result of this approach is that we have a wide spectrum of effectiveness and of size.

Some ministries are small because they need to be in order to be authentic and faithful. Like that great restaurant I spoke of earlier, what matters most is not the number of tables, but its distinctiveness and value to the city. Some microchurch ideas are more like boutiques serving a small population; others are designed to grow larger, and should be encouraged to do that. But even a philosophy of growth is something that should not be mandated. Additionally, all leaders are not the same. Some leaders are gifted in a way that gives them capacity to lead a larger mission, while others have a lower capacity and may never lead something large. We have to create a culture and language that celebrates growth of every kind and that celebrates faithful leadership instead of only tangible results. Who is to say that someone who leads hundreds is not actually operating below their potential and a person leading a boutique ministry of twenty people is not somehow exceeding it? Don't you think that God is probably measuring some metric other than just numbers? Likewise, we want to reward and celebrate, first, that people even try at all. This already makes them a minority group among American Christians. Second, we want to celebrate that they lead in a way that helps people to discover Jesus and helps his kingdom to come. These metrics are enough.

Our choice not to count the actual number of people involved in the microchurches is a deliberate and hopefully prophetic one that will allow us to stay true to what we do (namely, serve microchurches) and also to honor each work, whether large or small, as significant and equal to us. It keeps microchurches operating on a level playing field.

When a small microchurch asks for help creating a strategic plan or building a website or using the HUB, we make no distinction between them and the larger ones. We don't need to know precisely how many people are in these churches, because we don't want that information to bias our service to them. We celebrate the fruitful microchurches, but we never want to underappreciate the role of the smallest groups, because they all represent a risk taken and a calling obeyed. The irony here is that our use of the term "microchurch" is often inaccurate, as some of them grow quite large—perhaps even to the macro level. Yet, we persist in using this term because, to us, to emphasize the small is good in our culture that too often emphasizes the big. We offer that moniker as a term of endearment and a leveling word.

I recognize that our growth story is not fantastic, but that's the point. It's not incredible, but it's real, and it's significant in the kingdom of God. It is this modest yet significant growth in the face of an attempt to keep our work quiet that proves an important point. I do not offer our story as the latest trend or craze to be copied, but as research to be studied and validated for its timeliness, relevance, and weight.

I mean to stir those in leadership to godly jealousy and to open a dialogue about how some of these discoveries can be implemented in dying or hungry churches. I mean to awaken the imagination of Christians who sit in churches every week pondering the sad ineffectiveness of it all. And I mean to empower the person reading this who has long wondered if they were created for more, or if an idea they have long harbored is actually worth trying. You are—and it is.

INNOVATION AND SPIRITUAL WARFARE

One of the ways we express our mission as a network is, "to engage evil in all its forms." The UNDERGROUND is very much made up of people who have picked a fight with the devil. It is part of our apostolic culture to understand that any foray into the work of mission is necessarily warfare. Massive strongholds like addiction, homelessness, unbelief, violence, mental illness, prostitution, racism, and poverty are all ancient battlefields. They are not for the faint of heart and certainly not for the self-centered. But they are the right place for us. We clutch with white knuckles the declaration of Jesus that his people are the light of the world. Still, stepping on that battlefield is one thing; coming away with victory is quite another. We are brave enough to go, but the work of winning these battles remains elusive to many. That's why we need each other as we innovate and take new land for the kingdom.

I am not sure if anyone else has made the connection between innovation and spiritual warfare, but I am convinced they are related. Every day, we see the power of Jesus's name at work to free the addict or the abused. But we rarely see real progress in the battle against addiction or abuse itself. Supercharged by new technology, old evils find new dynamism in our world. Those of us who want to combat those trends and who believe that we are meant to be the salt of the earth preserving it and fighting against its decay are left with increasing complexity in our struggle.

We are desperate for fresh insights and innovation that will aid in confronting the changing face of evil in our time. For example, we have three microchurches that currently work to oppose the evil of human trafficking. They need innovative strategies to touch every layer of the problem. It is not enough to work only with the women who are affected; we also need to discern the kingdom come in the making of new laws. In a case like this, innovation is spiritual warfare.

Most people like the idea of innovation, but when it comes to seeing it nurtured and cultivated in the context of the church, we find few examples. Innovation takes the courage and willingness to question and eventually to let go of conventional operating principles. The church is notoriously bad at this. If I am right—that innovation is tied to effective spiritual warfare—then our rigidity is holding back the cause of Christ in the world. Innovation is at the forefront in our spiritual battle, because making the necessary changes threatens the enemy and ushers in the kingdom a little more.

In order to encourage this innovation, we first have to create environments where everything not established as theologically or biblically essential is open for examination. We have to rekindle the fire of the prophets in our communities and not hold them at arm's length or, worse, banish them for questioning our treasured traditions. We have to reward not only their questions, but also those who test their questions with alternate theories and experimental practice.

In simpler terms, if you have someone in your church community who is critical of something, embrace that *and them*. Press them to try an alternative. Say, "If this is wrong, then how should we do it?" And challenge them, "Will you do that? Will you lead?" Even further, once they have committed to lead, ask them, "How can I help you do that?" The true prophet will take that challenge and test the new theory. If they are wrong, what is lost except their pride? If they are right, we have everything to gain. And if, as we might suspect, they only want to criticize, then they will not follow through. Again, nothing is lost.

I am not saying just let them do whatever they want, I am

saying resource them to do what they envision. Anyone who has the vision to see new possibilities and the courage to pursue them should be given the full resources of the community to chase the work of God. Because the UNDERGROUND has made this simple choice to say "yes" to everyone, we find ourselves reaping a harvest of creativity and innovation.

One of the best things about the UNDERGROUND is that it is a home for prophets. Far from being a problem or a challenge to the system, they are welcomed and held accountable to their convictions. It has been a home for me as a prophet and has been a crucible in which my own assumptions can be tested, where my ideas can live on or die in the fire of living witness.

INNOVATION BEGETS INNOVATION

Jesus said, "From everyone who has been given much, much will be demanded; and from the one who has been entrusted with much, much more will be asked,"[4] and "To everyone who has, more will be given."[5] Watching the UNDERGROUND grow, I have come to believe that God has given his people incalculable creativity, vitality, and authority to carry out his mission in the world. We have been given so much, and so much is, therefore, required of us. Unfortunately, the prevailing narrative is that everyday Christians are not mature enough to lead or to innovate. This is a shame and, in my view, generally untrue. To us, who have been given so much, even more will be given. There is some principle of compound returns on creativity, innovation, and perhaps even virtue.

Creating this kind of environment for innovation and risk ends up spawning more innovation. Steven Johnson, in his amazing book *Where Good Ideas Come From*, explains that breakthroughs in any field do not happen like a light turning on but through a process more like building something from spare parts. Invention, he says, is a function of the spare parts with which you start.

Although the idea for it existed in his mind, Alan Turing could not build the World Wide Web, because the parts did not yet exist. Breakthroughs in inventing come only from using what is nearby, what Johnson calls "the adjacent possible."[6] In other words, nothing is ever totally new; it is built from the spare parts of previous inventions. Progress then is dependent on the breakthroughs that precede it. Our own church form/innovation, for instance, is only possible because of the adjacent possible of the Filipino church, the church in Antioch, the Franciscans, the Moravians, Luther, Wesley, the liberationists, the Pentecostals, et al.

We have discovered that, in the church world, if you can create an environment of experimentation and innovation, it not only attracts iconoclast inventors, it actually transforms everyone into innovators. When we think about missionary engagement through the lens of the adjacent possible we see that it is not just technique that can be improved from this kind of collaborative environment, but it is access to new ideas that improves the whole group.

For example, when one microchurch started doing late-night outreach on a street notorious for prostitution, their intention was to work with women caught in the snare of prostitution. They felt called to reach these women and, over time, to build a series of services not only to introduce them to Jesus, but also to take them by the hand and lead them away from the sex industry. Yet, as they went out night after night, they realized that not everyone they met was a woman. Some of the people walking those streets are transgender men. As they met these men, they discovered a new need and a new population for whom Christ died.

Later, a team of leaders came to us with a burning, unshakable sense of calling to the trans community, particularly those who were most vulnerable. We introduced this new missionary community to the first, and they began talking about collaborating in their street outreach. In a case like this, at the minimum, the first group can give the men they are meeting the phone number of some people who are eager and willing to walk them into their freedom.

This is an example of the adjacent possible. This story happens over and over in different variations at the UNDERGROUND. It has happened maybe hundreds of times in our network. It is impossible to measure the adjacent possible, but from my observation, we are swimming in it. As rich as our environment is for this kind of interaction, I still feel like we are not near where we need to be. We need more. The church needs more. It is this kind of collaboration—missionaries building off each other's work—that is missing from our church and missionary silos. Collaboration has eluded us because we do not entrust our work to each other.

When I think about collaboration between churches or Christian agencies, I typically imagine them working together on an established project, which is rare enough. However, innovative communities generate a kind of broader scale collaboration, not on an existing ministry effort, but on the greater goals of reaching and transforming the city—that more supernatural goal of reaching every nation and every unreached group of people.

Ironically, what should, and can still, unite us is not so much the things we have in common, but the places we have failed to reach. The goal of seeing the kingdom come to our cities must supersede all other goals. This drive for innovation is also the drive for the life and advancement of the kingdom itself.

Multiplying Mission Contexts

The final metric is difficult to track. How should we measure the coming of the kingdom of God? For example, how many orphans are in your city? How many people are homeless? What are your crime statistics? And of course, how many people have trusted Jesus and put their faith in him? Any change of those numbers toward the moral good should be a cause for celebration and a reflection of our prayerful action in our cities. Likewise, if those numbers are moving in the wrong direction, it should be cause for repentance and reflection. If we focus more on the metrics of the kingdom, and not just the results of our own work, then we will be more inclined to celebrate the work of any and all of Jesus's people, not just of paid staff members of churches.

In *Blue Ocean Strategy*, W. Chan Kim posits that the simplest way to start a profitable business is to move away from highly competitive environments by doing something that no one else is doing. If you start a business in uncontested market space—what he calls the "blue ocean" space—then you will be the only game in town.[7] Cornering the market is as simple as finding a market where no one is selling what you have to offer. The church doesn't need to keep battling for contested market space when there is a blue ocean out there. What we need, though, is the vision and imagination to see it.

Churches struggle to understand this. Perhaps the greatest failure of the church in my lifetime has been a failure of imagination. We keep competing for the same space in "the market," if the marketplace is the world out there. Even when we think about church growth or church planting (which is rare enough), we suffer from a staggering lack of imagination. Warren Bird says that the growing churches in North America typically grow because the neighborhoods they are in are growing, but these churches usually grow at a rate lower than the growth of the neighborhood.[8] In other words, for most growing churches, growth is an illusion. My thesis is that this is true because churches are failing to step into the blue ocean of mission. Even growing churches are losing, not gaining, ground.

Worse yet, our lack of imagination creates a culture and a spirit of competition between churches. We not only fail to find our way into the places of greatest need, but we fight with each other over the minority demographic that is already predisposed to come to a church service. So we go on planting more churches that compete with already existing churches for the people who are going to come to church one way or another. Yet, the uncontested mission space is left untouched, because we most often do not even think of another way to do church, let alone act on new ideas.

I have lived in the same inner-city neighborhood for twenty years. When I moved in, property values were the lowest in the city and violent crime rates were the highest in the city. We were the first family (that I am aware of) to move into this particular neighborhood for the kingdom's sake. To be sure, there were already kingdom people there, but we were the first to move in for the specific purpose of kingdom come. Over the past two decades, forty or more communities and households have chosen our neighborhood over all the other places to live in Tampa. The people of the UNDERGROUND have shown a special love to this part of the city, and they pour themselves out for its redemption. I have raised six children here, and while there have been challenges, I love my neighborhood and my neighbors with my whole heart. I cannot imagine living anywhere else.

During the time we have lived in our neighborhood, the crime rate has gone down by 82.1 percent.[9] Are we taking credit for that? Of course not. There are 100 mitigating factors for statistics like that. And yet, shouldn't we celebrate? Isn't this an answer to prayers and an outcome we believe the living church should deliver? While we do not take the credit, we should own the outcome. It is exactly what we have been living and laboring to see, and it is very much a sign of the kingdom.

So does all this work? The number of communities doing heroic mission work grows every year in our city. This was accomplished starting with the smallest group of underserved missionary innovators. We have empowered innovators and created a community that multiplies creativity. We have planted real churches, cared for the poor, made disciples, and seen previously unknown mission fields engaged. So if you care about those outcomes, then yes, it really works. And as much as the results excite me, the tangible experience of living this way excites me even more. Day to day, it is not the results that keep us going, but the culture of our church, which experiences life in the kingdom.

W|NDOW I

Aglimpse; a story about how these ideas play out in real life.

It's another hot Florida day. I check my calendar and see that I have a lunch meeting with Phil. I have met him only once, but he has been following our work at the UNDERGROUND and recently visited one of our Crucible gatherings. He reached out to me because he has an idea for mission. I am genuinely excited. I finish up a few emails as I see him through the window of my office. Everyone in the office is chatting him up, so I don't rush.

I come out, greet him, and ask if he's hungry. We take the quarter-mile walk from our offices to a burger restaurant called Fresh Mouth. This is my spot, the place of hundreds of meetings for me, meetings just like this one. It's a small space, surrounded by glass. It has an old '50s diner feel, with a lunch counter as its centerpiece. There is one booth in particular I like, so Phil and I find our way to it. Our waitress knows me so well that she just orders for me. I keep coming here because of the history I have with that booth. It is no exaggeration to say that I have helped dozens of ministries and served thousands of people, all starting in this booth—dreams, tears, prophecy, confessions, healing, revelation, so much goodness in this booth. For me, it is a holy place.

I ask Phil to tell me everything. I want to know as much of his life story as I can. I learn as much from how he tells the story, what he includes and what he leaves out, as I do from the details themselves. I am fascinated. People fascinate me—their stories, their resilience, their personalities, their idiosyncrasies. Ever since I came to believe that Jesus calls everyone into his mission, I see people differently. I look for that fire within them. I look for that beauty, that uniqueness, in every person. And I marvel at the way their gifts, their pain, their experiences, and their personality all coalesce into something totally and utterly special.

So, I get caught up in Phil's story. I finish my food before he has even taken a bite. Maybe he doesn't get listened to enough; I can't really tell. I like him, though. He starts to tell a version of the same story I have heard a hundred times in that same booth, a story about his own discovery of Jesus, about his initial love for the church, followed by frustration. These conversations always turn to talk about a burning passion for some underserved group of people, followed with a modest proposal for how the people of God could and should make a difference. I am all in.

I love it all so much. I love him for telling me the story. I love hearing it. I love him for the mirror he is holding up. I love him for witnessing to the stubborn and almost irrational way Jesus tries again and again to use human beings to do his work. I feel what I imagine a midwife feels. Though childbirth is anguish, strain, and hope for the mother, witnessing the process is all focus and wonder and encouragement. I want to help Phil do this.

I am not blind. I can see Phil has some obstacles and that he might not have a lot of experience leading a team or doing this kind of work. But I also hold in my mind a picture of the UNDERGROUND team back at the office, busy at work—all waiting for him to just ask for help before flooding his dream with competence, care, and community.

I start calculating the change in his life, in the world, and I can't hide my amusement. I crack a smile. But this isn't the right time for my mirth, so I hold back. He still has some angst and pent up frustration. I need to keep it together; I need to be empathetic. "I know what you mean," I say.

He tells me about asking a spiritual leader (it's usually a pastor, but it could be a parent or a group leader) about his idea. The person told him no because he wasn't ready, it was too hard, it wasn't the vision of the church . . . blah, blah, blah. I am starting to feel a little spark of anger in me, that old feeling I don't want to invite to the table of our lunch. But I see what is going on here, what is so often going on: Phil needs permission. He is looking for someone with some kind of organizational or spiritual authority to tell him he is allowed to love the poor, to reach the lost, to care for the uncared for. I push down the anger. I call on all my spiritual authority. I remember Jesus.

I tell him to put down his sandwich and look me in the eyes.

"You have permission. Do this, Phil. Give your life to it."

I can be intense sometimes. This is one of those times.

"It will bring you joy, and it will bring God pleasure. In fact, your heart for these people pleases him more than you will ever know. He loves you Phil, and he is calling you to love others. Yes, you should do this. Yes, *you can* do this."

I (half) jokingly make the sign of the cross over him to bless him.

I tell him I'm with him, that I will give him everything

I have to give, that I will marshal all the resources of the UNDERGROUND to help him do what needs to be done. I am with you; we are with you; we are behind you. Whatever you need—money, support, training, advocacy, mentoring, space—it's yours.

And now I know he is wondering what they all wonder. What is the catch? What do I have to do? So I cut to the chase and answer the question he has not yet asked, "No catch bro, no strings attached. I just want to help you do this."

He is speechless. I can see his eyes are stinging. He averts his gaze, wiping away his tears.

He finally says, "Thank you," I pick up the check, and we joke and make small talk as we walk back to the office, both of us pretending that it is just an ordinary day and that we just had an ordinary meeting.

Part 2

BRAVE PEOPLE

Chapter 6

OUR CULTURE

The opposite of a trivial truth is plainly false.
The opposite of a great truth is also true.

NIELS BOHR

The best thing about the UNDERGROUND is the people. Starting with the most committed has meant that impossible values and improbable reconciliation *are* possible. Dedicated, sacrificial, self-motivated, gracious, focused, and totally devoted to Jesus, these missionaries are hard to fully describe. In the same way that food is what really makes a restaurant great, so too are people what truly makes a church beautiful. This is good news, because in spite of all the structural flaws and failures traditional churches suffer, if the people are sincere reflections of Jesus, we might not notice. Love covers a multitude of sins. Structure influences culture, of course, but people who love Jesus, each other, and the world around them create a culture so strong that it supersedes structural problems. If you could only change one thing in a struggling church, you would want to change the culture.

The best definition I know for culture is, "the way we do things around here." Culture is not easy to identify and certainly is not easy to change in general, let alone in the church. It is something like poetry, really. Poems are structured, but that is not what we first notice about them, and in the end, it is not what makes us like them. Similarly, churches are structured, but that is not what we first notice about them, or what ultimately makes us want to stay. Like good poetry, the connection to a church's culture is more emotional. A poem is only effective to the degree to which it moves the reader.

Every poem can be understood as a balance of two facets: structure and texture.[1] Texture is the tangible detail of the poem; it is the lyrical style. Texture is the flesh, and structure is the bones. This serves as a great analogy for the two facets of church. Church culture is the texture, and the underlying systems and assumptions are its structure. The church is like living poetry. It is the Word of God in human flesh. We are supposed to be the body of Christ Jesus in the world, the incalculably beautiful Word made flesh. We are, like every poem, a balance of structure and texture. If culture is the texture, then it is the deep magic of a community dictating actions and attitudes without conscious thought. Culture can make difficult things easy to do, but it also can make seemingly simple changes arduous.

The culture of the UNDERGROUND is undeniably essential to its form and function, as it is to every church. And while a community as diverse as ours can be hard to categorize, there are some cultural qualities that seem to characterize almost every individual who has chosen to be part of it.

Playing with Paradox

To continue the comparison between church and poetry, Cleanth Brooks, as part of the New Criticism movement in the study of poetry, argues that all poetry is governed by both paradox and irony. He believes that all great poetry is principally expressing paradox or the "resolution of opposites."[2] I find this breathtaking. The longer I live and the more I try to interpret the deepest work of God in, through, and around me, the more I see the principle of poetic paradox at work in the way Brooks describes it. I think of Chesterton, the prince of paradox, who, in his final chapter of *Orthodoxy* called the "Ethics of Elfland," imagines God to be eternally young, having "the eternal appetite for infancy": ". . . for we have sinned and grown old, and our Father is younger than we."[3] This is the resolution of opposites, the vitality of youth and the wisdom of age reconciled in God.

Jesus's own teaching was filled with irony and paradox. "For whoever wants to save their life will lose it, but whoever loses their life for me will find it."[4] He can scarcely teach without it. He issues ironic statements like these often: the first are last, enemies are loved, the strong are weak, the greatest is the servant, death is life, the slave is free, the poor are rich and the rich are poor, the meek inherit the earth and persecuted are blessed, and the list goes on. The gospel itself is ironic. God dies for sinners; he is strong enough to be weak enough to die, so that we might live. The Nobel Prize-winning physicist Niels Bohr describes paradox this way, "There are trivial truths and there are great truths. The opposite of a trivial truth is plainly false. The opposite of a great truth is also true."[5] When I try to explain the culture of the UNDERGROUND—its texture—I have to speak in paradoxical terms. In other words, what's good about this community is like Double Dutch.

Double Dutch is a game played with two jump ropes being turned in opposite directions, with one or more players jumping in the middle. Double Dutch is mesmerizing to watch, not just because it requires skill, but also because of the songs and dances that go along with it. I think truth is often like a game of Double Dutch. There is not just one rope being navigated but, almost always, two. The two ropes go in opposite directions, and the only safe place to dance is right in the middle. Thinking of our lives as Christians in this way helps us to live in the tensions of paradox and irony. Are we, for instance, supposed to be content or discontent as Christians? Should we lament or laugh? Are we free in Christ or slaves of God? Is our core identity sinner or saint? Has the kingdom come, or is it coming later? Am I supposed to live an abundant life or die a martyr's death? Is the gospel something that is proclaimed or demonstrated? The answers to these questions are "yes." It's like Double Dutch—we play in the middle ground with two seemingly antithetical ropes swinging underneath us.

I think the UNDERGROUND embodies a culture of paradoxes. We are a little more comfortable with complexity than other groups, and we try to resist binary ideas that would tempt us to choose one way and not the other, because that black and white thinking tends to fragment us and bring us to war with each other. Here are six such tensions that we dance between:

1. Knowing and Not Knowing: A culture of experimentation.
2. Humility and Confidence: A culture of submission.
3. Prophetic and Personal: A culture of embodied protest.
4. Unity and Diversity: A culture of respect and missional priority.
5. Life and Death: A culture of passion and suffering love.
6. Clouds and Fire: A culture of practical dreamers.

Knowing and Not Knowing: A Culture of Experimentation

We have never abandoned the language of experimentation to describe our community, and there is real grace in that. If you see your work as an ongoing experiment, then you will feel a certain kind of liberation from achieving results. You'll be free to learn from the process. This is called organizational humility—there is always more to learn. You know, yet you don't know, but at least you know that you don't know.

Stroke patients who suffer from hemiplegia experience paralysis on one side of their body. Extraordinarily, the patients often don't know it. Even though they can't move one side of their body, they think they can. This condition is called anosognosia, the term of which comes from the Greek word *agnosis*, meaning lack of knowledge.

Leaders suffer from this condition, and churches too. They suffer from paralysis without even being aware of their issue. As the axiom goes, "We don't know what we don't know." The only solution is to crave and honor learning above "success." Because we see our attempts to recreate the church in the image of a missionary God, we have learned that learning is always a reward. But you have to be smart enough to admit what you don't know in order to reap the rewards.

Let me tell you a story to illustrate how blind we can be to our own paralysis. One morning in 1995, a Pittsburg man named McArthur Wheeler decided to rob not one, but two banks. He did so without a mask because he had become utterly convinced that lemon juice makes things invisible to modern cameras. He even tested this hypothesis by taking a selfie with his Polaroid camera. For some reason, the picture he took did not develop, so he was convinced. After rubbing generous amounts of lemon juice on his face, Wheeler proceeded to rob the banks. Looking directly and confidently into the banks' security cameras ultimately became his undoing, as police broadcasted his very visible face on the news. By day's end, Wheeler was in custody. Incredulous, the lemon juice bandit could not understand how the police were able to identify him. To the very end, he did not believe in his own ignorance.

This story caught the attention of two researchers, David Dunning and Justin Kruger. They wanted to understand the relationship between extreme ignorance and sublime confidence. They would go on to demonstrate that the less competent a person is, the more likely they are to exaggerate their own competence. In other words, the less we know about something, the less we realize our own ignorance. The phenomenon became known as the Dunning-Kruger effect.[6] Dunning wondered, "If Wheeler was too stupid to be a bank robber, perhaps he was also too stupid to know that he was too stupid to be a bank robber—that is, his stupidity protected him from an awareness of his own stupidity."[7]

Leaders, churches, and individuals threaten their own mission and values by simply failing to understand the limits of their own understanding and competence. This corporate anosognosia is crippling the effectiveness of the church. The irony here is that it takes courage and wisdom to realize and admit what we don't know. It takes courage to explore the limits of our own experience and knowledge thoroughly enough to face its insufficiency. We decided to integrate and champion the tension between knowing and not knowing at the UNDERGROUND. That two-toned texture is our built-in way of staying humble. In the end, humility is smart. In fact, it is part of what makes us brave.

Humility and Confidence: A Culture of Submission

Embracing our life's mission as an experimental process helps us to embrace the most potent of all virtues, what Andrew Murray calls "the root of all virtue,"[8] humility. Humility graces all it touches—the people, the systems, the organization, and even the culture. It not only humbles us, it also empowers us. This kind of willingness to do something imperfectly only reinforces that God himself can be trusted—in all things. We are not confident in our own insight or our own opinion, but we cling to things like the Scripture, the gospel, and the testimony of the Holy Spirit in us. We are bold precisely because we are willing to be wrong. We are sure of the kingdom exactly because we are not so sure of ourselves. Our confidence grows as we experiment, because we see God working amidst our "failures." We try and fail, listen and learn because the mission of God is more important than anything else. It's more important because my pride and my need to be right is nothing compared to the world's need for justice and lost souls' need for heaven.

At its heart, humility is about God. It is about surrender and submission to him. Submission to God necessarily means openness to hearing him in the world and in the people around us. It means we could always be wrong, and so we search and listen. Maybe the greatest gift our culture of experimentation affords is humility. We are learning every day at the UNDERGROUND. There is a culture of submission to that process. We enter every new mission context with the conviction that we do not fully understand it or know exactly what is needed, and therefore we arm ourselves with questions instead of answers, and curiosity instead of prescriptions, while still calling on our prior experiences and knowledge. This kind of personal humility translates into organizational humility, which is a joy to experience within a group. We are freed from the tyranny of perfectionism, along with the nagging demands of performance and the expectation that we should already know the answer. If scorn is the intolerance of weakness and stupidity in others, ignorance is the intolerance of weakness and stupidity in ourselves. At our most foolish, we prefer ignorance to knowledge because it is simply too hard to believe that the way we look at the world could be fundamentally flawed, or that we ourselves are flawed. It takes real strength and, ironically, even confidence to admit what we don't know. This is why the hyper-religious and overeducated had trouble with Jesus. He exposed ignorance in them that they were not prepared to believe existed.

W.H. Auden wrote, "We would rather be ruined than changed, we would rather die in our dread than climb the cross of the moment and let our illusions die."[9] This may be especially true of our illusions about our own competence, but the converse is just as true and just as liberating. If we will be ruined by healthy change, if we are willing to die to our pride in the pursuit of Jesus and his mission, then we are truly free.

So we lift our voices and lay down our lives, knowing that we are sinners too. We seek the salvation of the world, and in the process, we too are saved. I think this is what Andy Crouch means when he talks about human flourishing being (ironically) the simultaneous pursuit of authority and vulnerability.[10] It is what comes from this culture of submission to God and openness to him in the people and world around us. It is the ironic blend of humility and confidence, strength from weakness, certainty from questioning. His beautiful book *Strong and Weak* is perfect for further reading on what this paradox can look like in a community's culture. And it is a principle the UNDERGROUND has always (albeit imperfectly) embraced.

Prophetic and Personal: A Culture of Protest

As part of our culture, we balance both the prophetic and the personal aspects of life in the kingdom. We share a common desire to challenge and even protest the evil we see in the world. That evil takes up residence in people and systems, but also in us. So while we carry in us a culture of protest, that protest is not just externalized; for it to be valid, it must also be applied to our own sin.

When it comes to politics, for instance, the people of the UNDERGROUND are neither Democrats nor Republicans. According to our Twitter analytics—for whatever that is worth— the political affiliation of our affiliates is split, 50–50. I am sure our people vote, and because we are forced into the two-party dualism of the American electoral system, they vote for one or the other. If asked about voting, many, if not most, would resist the question. I think we would not want to be in either category, not because we are necessarily apolitical, but because we actually see some merits to both positions, as well as the errors of both positions. Still, we are active. We will walk in protests, are vocal on issues, and vote our conscience, but without demagoguery or dogma. It is the paradox of protest.

Probably about half of us are Reformed and half are Wesleyan. We have some people who are Complementarian and some who are Egalitarian. Just over half our leaders are people of color.

Instead of a certain *political* stance, the UNDERGROUND culture is defined by certain *prophetic* stances. This means that we pick fights, and at the same time, we treasure humility—in ourselves and in others. We want people to stand up for something, for Jesus: for justice, for the poor, for righteousness, for the gospel. Yet, we also recognize that we are flawed human beings. While our hearts and hands are ready to fight for those signs of the kingdom, we also know we sin in the process. We are, I think, even in our own call for repentance, ready to repent ourselves. We are, in our call for justice, ready to become more just. We are ready to see the evil in our own hearts as we decry the evil in the world. It is possible to embrace truth in a way that is both prophetic (external) and personal (internal). Jesus doesn't say we should not help our brother to get the splinter out of his eye; he said only to get the log out of ours first. Prophecy must be preceded by an embodiment of the call being made. In the midst of the personal and prophetic, we also remember a time when we ourselves neither knew nor obeyed the truths we proclaim.

Unity and Diversity: A Culture of Respect and Missional Priority

One of the great challenges for the church in the twenty-first century is to embrace and embody the multiethnic vision God has for his people. From the prayer he taught us to pray, we learn to hunger for expressions of heaven in this life. Make it true on earth, we pray, as it is in heaven. And yet, that picture of heaven, which is made stunningly clear in Revelation 4 and 8, is that of a people unified not in their common language but in their common love for the king and his kingdom. This vision from Revelation—and what we pray to come to earth—is still a far cry from what it looks like on Sunday mornings.

Yet, multiethnicity is one of those pursuits that seems to strain and struggle under its own weight. When the church makes a direct campaign to be more multiethnic, it often comes off as tokenistic or as neo-objectifying, particularly when a majority culture church tries to "include" people of different ethnicities and backgrounds. It might be a noble desire, but oftentimes, the execution only alienates people more and deepens the divide that was already there.

There has been an encouraging trend toward multiethnicity in recent years. Still, being able to grow and nurture a truly multiethnic church or organization remains an elusive goal. Those who have experienced it know it is full of extraordinary value and that it is always under attack. There is a never-ending barrage of threats to the fragile life of a multiethnic community. Maintaining a theology of ethnic diversity merely in one's head is not enough to hold people together, because while we may all agree that the church should be a representation of heaven—a multilingual, multinational, and multicultural affair—living that out is another story.

If the UNDERGROUND has anything to add to this deeply important conversation, it must be tied to our emphasis on empowerment and mission. When we say we will give free services and become a family to anyone who is willing to join the mission in our city, this creates an invitation and open door not only to reach every ethnicity, but to serve every kind of leader. We have found people who are either already doing that kind of work (and are attracted to that proposition) or those who want to take up the task. The missionary niche will have representation from every ethnicity, because God himself is the one who calls and God "shows no favoritism."[11] His perfect valuation of human worth is reflected in the free distribution of his authority.

We have discovered that by helping people find their calling, then responding, we can organize our resources very differently. Likewise, if churches would simply serve and empower people called into mission, then somewhere we would find that the result is a multiethnic community of drastically diverse people. Since there is diversity in mission, openness to mission necessarily means embracing diversity.

Ministries that serve the homeless, for instance, do not struggle to be multiethnic. Anyone and everyone with particular needs shows up because these ministries have defined their work as service to, for, and with those who have certain kinds of need. Hunger and homelessness do not befall only one ethnicity or culture. Ministries that provide food for the hungry will find that the population surrounding the table is almost always multiethnic. Likewise, if the church were defined and organized around serving mission, then we might find that the table we set for missionaries is also a multiethnic table.

We recently did a survey on all our ministry leaders and discovered that 51 percent were people of color. Even more interesting, 66 percent were women. We did not set out to serve one ethnicity specifically, nor have we directly worked to only empower women, but when we act as though we really believe in the priesthood of all, and when we make ourselves available to everyone, diversity is the outcome.

That is not to say that we have not had to work at multiethnicity, and it's not to say that it doesn't take foresight and some cultural sophistication in order to receive diversity when it arrives. On the contrary, once people take us up on our offer of service we have found that, whatever the cultural starting point, we need to constantly evaluate and even repent from the ways the majority culture is advantaged. While service opens the door and mission creates a bond, a multiethnic family is not forged without great effort, humility, listening, repentance, and prayer. In the end, it is all worth it, and being on mission may be the only lasting solution to real diversity in the church. Every step and every sacrifice is worth it if the family that is formed carries in it the DNA of heaven.

The result is a new kingdom culture that honors every representation of the heart and glory of God in the world. Our microchurch leaders do not all agree on their preferences, but at a deeper level, there is mutual respect for the places we work and the people with whom we work because we are all pursuing the same vision for the kingdom of heaven. I am persuaded that only a multiethnic community will adequately witness to this generation and capture their imagination. The challenges of creating a more diverse church community are small compared to the hope that diversity gives us.

Life and Death: A Culture of Love

Perhaps every Christian should be ready to lay down their life for the testimony of Jesus. When Jesus promised the church his presence, he also left them an identity as witnesses. The original word for witness in Greek, *martus*, is where we get the English word "martyr" because the witness Jesus was describing was a matter of life and death. In our lives, there are some people and even ideas that we are so deeply committed to, toward which we feel such profound love, that we would be willing to suffer and even die for them. Jesus calls for that kind of love, not just for him, but for each other and, perhaps more to the point, for the world that rejects us. We are his witnesses precisely because we are willing to die like him in the service of lost people. Our people are witnesses in this sense. They have decided to lay down their lives, their careers, their names, and their futures for the sake of this great love.

In 1951, Salvador Dali debuted what would become his most famous religious painting, *Christ of St. John of the Cross*, so named because it was inspired by a sketch made by St. John of the Cross, the sixteenth-century Spanish friar. At first, it was critically reviled. But within a period of two weeks, thousands had stood in line to see it. One press report about this sketch read, "Men entering the room where the picture is hung instinctively take off their hats, crowds of chattering high spirited school children are hushed into awed silence when they see it."[12] What makes the painting remarkable is its point of view. It is a depiction of the crucifixion from above. It is, presumably, God's view of the event.

Paul Althaus wrote, "Jesus died for God before he died for us."[13] The act of dying is also an act of obedience, love, and worship. Jesus himself would say that unless a seed falls to the ground and dies, it cannot bear fruit.[14] So it is that death and life are linked in the Christian journey. We must be willing to die both metaphorically and actually in order to see the kingdom of God in our lives. If anyone would come after me, Jesus explains, they "must deny themselves and take up their cross daily and follow me."[15]

Dali's painting draws us anew into the idea of the cross as a thing of beauty and not horror. His portrait has no blood or gore, and the agony on the face of Jesus is obscured. It is less realistic than some portrayals, but it nevertheless makes an important point— God's view of the cross would have been different than ours.

In *The Message of the Cross*, Derek Tidball writes, "Before the cross countless men and women of every generation and culture have stood in adoring wonder and humble penitence. The cross stands at the very heart of the Christian faith, manifesting the love of God, effecting salvation from sin, conquering the hostile forces of evil and inviting reconciliation with God."[16]

The topic of the first sermon I ever preached (when I was sixteen years old) was the crucifixion. That sermon, as I look back now, is like a stake driven into the landscape of my theology. It represents my understanding of God, to which I am tethered and from which I can never stray too far. I think it is the same for the culture of the UNDERGROUND. Our people celebrate the table and embody this paradox of life through the death of Christ every time they gather. When we are all together on the weekends, we always share communion. The cross holds us together and always brings us back—to ourselves, to each other, and to the sacrificial love of Jesus. Communion is the fullest expression of this paradox because it is a time of both celebration and lament. It is a place of sadness and repentance (death), as well as joy and freedom (life). We are a people of the cross, defined by the suffering of Jesus, and each of us is not only ready to suffer but to celebrate those who suffer for his sake and in his name. We do not chase this suffering, but we also will not run from it. It looks like passion and zeal. It is a culture of tangible love. When we follow Jesus, we follow him to the cross. He who was sent was sent to die. That was the fullness of his mission.

Clouds and Fire: A Culture of Practical Dreamers

The image of clouds and fire comes from the story of Israel. For them, the presence of God was a matter of life and death. The permanence of the Temple was not always a reality, because for so much of their history, Israel was a people on the run. In more nomadic times, God revealed himself in the tabernacle, a kind of portable temple that could be packed and moved with them. Even though this tent was full of sacred things, none of them mattered unless Yahweh manifested himself through it all. The reality of his presence meant life, justice, protection, and hope for this people in search of a home. He was their home on the journey, and his visible presence was the confirmation of all he had promised them. In this mystical story, God was visible to his people in the form of both clouds and fire. These two very different and very potent images show that he confirmed his promises; he led his people; and he went with them.

He still does.

Here's what I mean: clouds are pieces of the sky. They are not practical—they are spiritual, ethereal, and a part of heaven. They aren't earthy. When we talk about dreamers and visionaries, we often say their heads are in the clouds, presumably meaning they are not considering cold, hard reality but are living in the sky. Clouds are unpredictable. They inspire wonder and remind us of our dreams. The leadership of God is somehow like the clouds. Yet, that image is not enough. He is also like fire.

There is scarcely a more powerful element in the ancient world than fire. It is from the earth—real and practical. It's required for work to be completed: meals cooked, cold dispelled, and waste consumed. Fire is about burning; it is heat, but it is also light. It does not just drive away the bitter cold; it also dispels the beleaguered darkness. It is light, dangerous light. To use it, hold it, or employ it is to risk pain and destruction. Fire is adventure and passion, risk and reward. God seems to want us to stand with our heads in the clouds and our feet in the fire.

To live like this means, on the one hand, that we have to find a way to dream again. We have to dream dreams big enough for God. The God who fills the small spaces of our lives is the same God whose glory covers the earth. That is the God to whom our dreams rise up. We keep our heads in the clouds where God reigns, where death dies, where there is no sickness, no abuse, and no captivity. The Lord's Prayer is the prayer of a starry-eyed dreamer.

We dream to bring what we see in the heavens here to earth. Together, all God's people's dreams start to complete the picture of the dream of God. The UNDERGROUND is a collection of

God-inspired dreams. These are dreams of the kingdom coming in the lives of black girls and boys, vulnerable women, young adults exiting the foster care system, men and women with addictions, lost students on university campuses, homeless teens, spouses of marriages in distress, Haitian immigrants, Chinese international students, women in prison, countless neighbors in countless neighborhoods, migrant farm workers, individuals with disabilities, families with special needs, people with mental illnesses, community college students, kids without advocates, and the list goes on.

A key to our culture at the UNDERGROUND is that we love to nurture dreams. Hand in hand with these dreams, we embrace the paradox of fire. We are a people comfortable with fire. That is, we burn and obsess over God's agenda in this world. We fight and struggle; we contend and wrestle; we yearn and hunger. We are a people on fire, who feel, who have compassion, who carry righteous anger, fierce loyalty, and dogged commitment to their grave. We're not perfect, but this is who we strive to be.

There are those who dream, but do not do; there are those who work, but never wonder. This is the paradox of the culture of the church that has its head in the clouds and its feet in the fire. We must be idealists *and* realists. We must be principled *and* practical.

This is life, life to the fullest, life in the presence of God. This is a vision of his people possessed by his dream and consumed with his passions. This chapter—maybe even this whole book—is a kind of tribute to the people of the UNDERGROUND, ordinary people who show me time and time again that this kind of church culture is possible and very real.

Chapter 7

SURPRISES

There is still, for me, no pathos quite like the pathos of those multicolored, worn, somehow triumphant and transfigured faces, speaking from the depths of a visible, tangible, continuing despair of the goodness of the Lord. I have never seen anything to equal the fire and excitement that sometimes, without warning, fill a church, causing the church . . . to rock.

JAMES BALDWIN

The value of an experiment is in what we learn from it. True experimentation is about discovery. Whether an assumption is proved or disproved, a true experiment will always lead to discovery and learning. Many of our theories at the UNDERGROUND have been validated through experimentation, some of which I have shared in this book, but there were surprises too. Some of these surprises had to do with forces beyond our control, and some are the direct result of either our failure or our faithfulness. Some have to do with sin, and others can only be attributed to the grace of God. When I think through them all, there are the six that I believe are significant enough to share here.

People Feel Called to More Than Just One Thing

All our microchurches are autonomous and have their own leaders or, in some cases, teams of leaders. In one sense, the core community of the UNDERGROUND is made up of these leaders. We have two rules that govern the basic ethics of this rich leadership community and their interactions with each other: there can be no cross-recruiting and no intra-organizational fundraising. In order to hold together our coalition, the UNDERGROUND has promised that ambitious leaders will not loot teams when those leaders are looking for fresh laborers. And since everyone has financial needs, we have to create a place where fundraising between teams is off limits. That doesn't mean one group can't give to another mission, just that no one can actively seek donations from other groups. This is something we've learned to implement over time. The people in our communities are free to give to whatever they want, and being surrounded by a myriad of missionary ventures gives every person many options.

Occasionally, one ministry will lose a promising leader to another microchurch. However, when the catalyst is not recruitment but a prompting from the Holy Spirit, or the free choice of that leader, we can all celebrate. We foresaw this dynamic and have tried to create an open-handed, generous culture that always submits to the voice of God. What is more remarkable—and this came as a surprise to us—is not that people choose one ministry over another, but that they end up just being a part of both.

When the UNDERGROUND was just being formed, I was influenced by the house church movements of the past. I was captured by the viral quality of these movements, the way they simplified and democratized practices so that they could grow exponentially. I still have great honor for that simple type of church and would welcome it in my own city. The limitation for this kind of cellular church model, however, is that it does not allow for diversity of ideas or expressions. A house church movement, then, is a movement of house churches, not orphanages or street preachers or abolitionist teams or a thousand other expressions of the kingdom, which cannot be contained or carried by a house church. We decided that these and other models of cellular replication are beautiful but incomplete. We learned that as we freed people to dream and follow Jesus into mission, the results were not homogenous. People wanted to do more than one kind of ministry.

In our case, we originally thought everyone would discern their calling, form or find a community that shared that calling, then pursue their life of mission together, contextualizing and learning as they went. That certainly has happened, but what we did not expect was that so many people would double dip in missions. Perhaps it represents a glitch in our limited definition of calling (one thing for life), or perhaps we underestimated the capacity of people's hearts to care about more than one issue. Any way you slice it, we have come to see that many of our most committed people do not participate in just one microchurch; they are often involved in two and sometimes even three.

Some of this cross-pollination is necessitated by collaboration. For example, the college student ministries often send teams to volunteer with the homeless ministries. Many would identify themselves as members of multiple communities. Another example is that the regional director for the local college ministry also has a heart for vulnerable women, so she goes on street outreach events with them every month. The woman who works with kids as they age out of foster care also serves with a group of mentors for other at-risk kids. They sit on each other's boards, serve across demographics, and in many cases, simply care about more than one issue.

Sometimes people choose to work in more than one mission because their calling is undeveloped; sometimes it is what they believe God has called them to do. For those still trying to figure out their calling and who they are, the options available for service in our interconnected microchurches allow them to discern what they might be willing to give their life to. They use their involvement in activism and service as a way of discerning their calling. Others know definitively that they are called to more than one thing, and so they make space in their life and work to serve both of those callings.

So Few Give Up

Another surprise related to the realization that people are sometimes called to more than one issue has been our remarkable lack of turnover. I say they are related, because I believe it is *the very fluidity of mission* that creates multiple loyalties that keep people in the game longer. Many of our people work with populations that are very difficult. Not only are the people difficult, but so too are the circumstances and stressors that surround them. For instance, one of our microchurches called "The Well" is working with the large homeless population in Tampa. They are constantly battling the corresponding demons of addiction, violence, mental illness, and general disregard by the city and its systems. The leaders of The Well are forever treading water, struggling not only to serve their people, but also to hold on to any kind of facility because, everywhere they go, their neighbors and the city itself wants them gone.

The burnout rate for social workers and inner-city missionary types is extremely high, and understandably so. Yet, I have been shocked at how low our turnover rate is. Don't get me wrong, microchurch ideas fail all the time; we lose between 10–20 percent of these groups every year. That is to be expected with any kind of start-up community. What we did not expect is that the same people who find the end of one idea simply move on to something else. They either find another microchurch to work with (one they may have already been serving) or they start something new. Many of our start-ups are recycling leaders from ideas that never took off. In other words, ideas fail in our network, but our people don't. There is something resilient about this community, and I think it might have something to do with the other leaders. People see that George is not giving up, Jon is not quitting, Jillian is staying with it, so they decide, *I will too*. And even when ideas come up short, that is no reason to give up on the dream of the kingdom. That is no reason to stop being and building the church. This, too, is a beautiful surprise.

When Missionaries Worship, It Is Utterly Different

We host a worship gathering on Sundays called Crucible—but not every week. We take off some weeks because we just need time off, and sometimes we take a week off because we want to join someone else for their worship gathering. And sometimes, we take a Sunday off for the same reason I had breakfast with my fiancée Monica on the morning of our wedding—because everyone says you can't.

One such Sunday, I asked all our staff members[1] to choose a church in our city to visit. We made a list of all the churches that had good reputations, and we each took one. My hope was that we would learn something from each experience. Because we had been almost reclusive, I was hoping we would gain some perspective on the work of God's people in the city and, hopefully, each of us would bring back something precious to strengthen or even correct our work.

The church I chose was pretty big, a little bit outside of town, sitting on a sprawling suburban plot. I had no problem finding it because the traffic was backed up for blocks. While there was visitor parking close to the church, I wanted to take my time, so I parked pretty far from the main building. This gave me time to experience the strangest sensation—nostalgia.

As I joined the throng of people making their way from the parking lot into the building, I felt a growing excitement. Maybe it was because I was trying something different or going somewhere new for the first time, but I had this unmistakable feeling of expectation. I have to say, it had been some time since I felt excited to go to a church service. There was also something about that long walk that triggered memories of going to church with my grandparents when I was a kid. I had that feeling like something important was about to happen. I began to really believe it. I was swelling with hope and faith. I was going to encounter God and stand in the midst of his people.

The sense was as beautiful as it was fleeting.

The place was sprawling. Not one person talked to me. I sat in some bleacher-like seats too far from the front to feel any kind of connection with the people on stage. I wasn't sure what to look at—the people or the screens. What I witnessed felt contrived and lifeless. Don't get me wrong, people were trying to make it something. Boy, were they trying. The incongruence between the indomitable smile of the worship team and the lifeless worshipers was hard to reconcile. The people on stage were like game show hosts, caricatures of choreographed happiness, while the crowd stood motionless and disinterested. There was an occasional zealot really trying to go for it, but even those people seemed out of place. I am sure they were genuine people, but what I'm describing was my perception. Not one bit of it seemed real to me. I quickly felt a deep sympathy for those smiling singers, because their audience was brutal. If I had been on stage, I would have wanted to throw down the mic and run off in tears.

I tried to close my eyes and worship the Jesus I know. Perhaps it is a defect in my character or it was my unfamiliarity with the place—or perhaps it was that no one around me was singing—but I found it very difficult to worship. Mercifully, the music ended. We were then subjected to a sermon before the sermon—about the offering. This was hard to deal with because I could feel the financial pressure, this mad grab to get more money to pay for the whole expensive fiasco. But I still held out hope for the preaching. And to be perfectly honest, it turned out to be fine. Serviceable.

Solid. I was mostly thankful for the reminder of a couple of truths that are always welcome. Still, in the end, my experience fell far short of my yearning.

I left facing that familiar task of managing my disappointment. So much of our experience with church among those at the UNDERGROUND is learning to manage disappointment, not so much in the shortcomings of human leaders, although that can be a challenge, but in the shortcomings of the collective encounter (or lack of encounter) with God. What is the church if not the tangible experience of the presence of God?

In *The Word of God, the Word of Man*, Karl Barth captures that singular moment when the preacher steps up to the lectern, pulls on the light, and opens the text. There is this hush, he says, a deep anticipation, a collective hope. Maybe, just maybe, this will be the time. Maybe we will hear today the voice of the living God. Maybe God will arrive in power and be heard, felt, and worshiped in the hearing of his voice. Maybe we will experience God in the midst of his people.[2]

Then, the inevitable letdown comes. Instead of that hope, we experience varying levels of soul disappointment. To be sure, some of us are more forgiving of this discrepancy than others. Some have learned to manage the disappointment well. *It was good*, we say to ourselves. *He did the best he could*, we say. We scrape and struggle for a few "takeaways," but mostly we know it was not what we had hoped. We can do it for a while, but eventually, we grow weary of the revisionist optimism and excuses. This frustration is really just a microcosm of the longing for the church itself.

Barth isolates that moment of preaching in his book, and that is fine. I want to see God then too, and he agrees that mostly we wait in vain for the presence of God to be manifest there. But it is much more often than in the moment of formal preaching when we long for the voice of God. I think we wake up each morning with the hope of the kingdom stubbornly nudging us. It is not just the light of the lectern coming on, but the dawning of each day, that makes us yearn for the presence of God to be manifest in our lives. Still, though, we manage the disappointment of not seeing the church in power, not seeing the church radiant with the living presence of God.

I have already made the case for structural change. I do not think we can change our experience of the church if we cannot address its framework and its operating model. Still, structures are only the flesh and form of a thing, not its beating heart. We could address and change every shortcoming in our church's form and still find the existential experience of the church devoid of God. Paul said it was possible to have a form of godliness (body politic) and yet to deny its power (spirit animation).[3] Paul expresses this theme again and again and applies it to different problems the church faces. In all cases, there is an implicit failure to present (in the form) the living presence of God.

So much of my experience of the church before forming the UNDERGROUND had become an exercise in managing disappointment. Yet, to my great surprise, I have had the opposite experience with the UNDERGROUND. Maybe that is because I feel responsible, or often because I am leading some part of it, but I think it is more than that. I am still cynical sometimes about us too. I still have that lingering doubt, the opposite of hope. It's what Brené Brown calls "foreboding joy."[4] Foreboding joy is when I think this will be the week that the Spirit of God abandons the whole thing or, more to the point, that we will fail to allow him to come. Only I come to find, week after week, tears of surprise and relief when he does come.

So what is it? I think it comes down to this: when missionaries worship, it is different than when nominal Christians worship. I don't think we have the best musicians or the most talented speakers, but there is a desperation and hunger that characterizes all our gatherings. I am surprised that this kind of deep perception of need has not diminished in us in all these years. You can still feel it every time we gather. Tears often punctuate our gatherings, so many tears. Our worship leaders break down; I often break down. Nothing is rote. All is new.

Maybe God always seems to be present because we express in our gatherings that we need him so much. Maybe it's because we don't have spectators; we only have participants. They don't come to watch; they come to find God. When you work with the very poor, you face constant betrayal and pain beyond your ability to bear it. When you spend the other six days a week face-to-face with real evil and you battle with all your strength to confront strongmen like unbelief, racism, prostitution, homelessness, and mental illness, it is all just too much. We know we need God. The people who gather to worship with us are spent. They don't come to judge or consume, they come to find a moment with the living God; they come to be touched by him, revived, and reminded of his promised presence. I am not sure if it is their hunger that invokes the presence of God or if it is their faithfulness. But I am reminded of the promise at the end of the Great Commission: go, make, teach, baptize . . . and surely I will be with you to the end of the age. Surely.

It is hard to face that statement as a conditional promise, but it is. That means the converse might hold true as well. Perhaps we can conclude that if we do not go, if we do not make disciples, if we do not baptize and teach people to obey all that Jesus has commanded, then his Spirit will not be as present with us.

It is like the indictment of the prophets: I hate your solemn assemblies, because you neglect the poor.[5] If we really believe Scripture, then we have to face the very real possibility that our experience of church, where the majority of people have neglected the poor and have refused to make disciples, might mean the withdrawing of the tangible presence of God from our gatherings.

Likewise, if we only obey those living mandates, no matter

how good or bad our music or preaching, he has promised to be with us. Somewhere inside us, the spirit of Jesus searches for connection with his bride, for communion with his people. We are all hoping to see the church alive, visible, real, whole, potent, and formidable.

I think two decades of managing disappointment with the church made me doubt if the presence of God was really something I could consistently expect and count on. I still struggle with that doubt. Yet, this strange band of missionary people has slowly healed and rewired my expectations to believe in the reliable manifest presence of God.

True Diversity Is Fragile and Always Under Attack

At times, it has been hard to hold us together. The work of the enemy is fragmentation. He cannot create or build; all he can do is dismantle, alienate, and tear apart. Conversely, it is the deepest work of God in the world to restore, reconcile, and reunite. God is reconciling all things, because all things are estranged, not only from him, but also from each other. There are powers and principalities at work in this world that I do not claim to understand, but I do experience their work of shattering and breaking.

In many ways, the UNDERGROUND is a great attempt to reconcile the church back to its identity and its purpose. It is an attempt to reconcile Christians to each other through the preeminence of calling and mission. It is not one church but a family of churches, a coalition of creative and autonomous churches that have a million reasons to resist their affiliation with each other.

We are trying to empower every kind of person in every kind of context to reach every kind of person in every kind of context. We give away power and serve people who are pursuing that great mission. The result is a multiethnic, multi-ideological, and multidoctrinal community. Everything human beings break relationships over, we try to reunite under the banner of the supremacy of God in mission. To say that this work attracts spiritual attack is an understatement. Our desire to see the boundaries of the kingdom expand, particularly into the places and among people where the church has not gone, has painted a bull's-eye on our backs.

Further, we have a desire to empower people who are orthodox Christians but who are also politically liberal and conservative, Calvinist and Wesleyan, Complementarian and Egalitarian, black and white, middle class and poor, old and young, native and immigrants—and all of those polarities pull at our people without ceasing and without mercy. In all these dichotomies, there is always pain and misunderstanding, always a minority position. There is always a place where power has traditionally resided. So, while our work is to unite and to hold together the fragile peace that mission creates, it is also to side with the weakest and to speak truth to power. This, too, has its perils.

I have been honest about just how beautiful this community really is, but I also have to be honest and admit to myself every day that this beauty is under attack and often marred by sin, fear, and misunderstanding. We have lost face, lost sleep, and lost people because some of these strongholds prove to be too much for a particular relationship. Sometimes I feel like the whole of this world is working against us. As if mission work against the unbelief and evil of this world was not hard enough, we also must undertake the perilous work of healing divisions that have infected the church.

All this is to say that I have been surprised that encouraging and maintaining diversity is much harder than I expected, but in turn, the unity we have achieved is that much more miraculous. I think of our black leaders as an example. Every day, it seems there are reasons for these remarkable leaders to back out. They face so much difficulty and trauma in this country, a country that still does not fully value their lives, their gifts, their dignity, and their contributions. Why would they persevere in a multiethnic church context (with white people) when that experience has been so full of threat and danger for them? And yet they do. They stay.

"Where sin increased," Paul wrote, "grace increased all the more."[6] These leaders are a constant reminder to me that love hopes, perseveres, and keeps no record of wrongs. I would not find fault in these leaders if they just wanted to retreat into the security and honor of the strong and beautiful black church. They have an alternative to this multiethnic vision and community, but still they see the kingdom represented in our trying. More than anything, they are missionaries who want to see the kingdom come. It is the hope of heaven, I think, that keeps them engaged. The minority people in every polarity we face experience this dynamic, to varying degrees. Everyone, at one time or another, will have to show the same courage and the same vision that these leaders have shown.

There Is Almost No Pettiness or Politics in Missional Communities

The upside of working with the most committed 20 percent of people in the church is the relative absence of pettiness, which is the next major surprise I have seen with the UNDERGROUND. Of course, I cannot speak for all churches everywhere, but it seems that the North American church has a bit of a reputation for trifling and politics. I had hoped it would be different for us when we started. I believed that by focusing on something more significant than our differences and our petty grievances against each other we might be immune to that kind of thing. And to my surprise, it has turned out to be just that way.

I had a friend who was gently trying to lead his church away from a few dead traditions and into what he believed was a more biblical kind of church. He dreaded Mondays because there were always one or two emails in his in-box criticizing his sermon from that weekend. It was as regular as it was discouraging. I confess, I carried a latent fear of that kind of scrutiny finding its way into our community. In ten years of preaching (almost weekly) to our gathering of hundreds of missionaries, I have never received an email like that.

Don't get me wrong—I have said plenty of things that could have (and maybe even deserved) criticism. I often go off script and occasionally (maybe once every few months) say something even I regret—not to mention the questionable things I don't regret but which I know will rub people the wrong way. As a comparison, I would say my friend was exponentially more careful and gentle in his challenges to his people, and still, his leadership was riddled with constant criticism.

So, if it is not the preaching itself that can be blamed or credited for the response, then what is it? It would be simple to say that UNDERGROUND people are just more mature. But instead, I would offer the notion that they are too focused on their own leadership, their own desperation, and their own need for God to bother me with criticism. A critical spirit takes time and energy to nurture. The truth is, our people are just too tired for all that. Their lives have enough drama that they don't feel the need to add more of it to our regular gatherings.

One of my favorite books on marriage is written by Francis and Lisa Chan. It's called *You and Me Forever.* The book is a bit of bait and switch because it is less about marriage and more about surrender to the supremacy of God.[7] They argue that we will have better marriages not by trying to have better marriages—the emphasis and focus of which can actually become idolatry—but by being better disciples. It is the triangulation of submission to Jesus that draws couples closer together. This principle holds true for all relationships, and I could not agree with it more. Not only would our marriages be experientially better and endure longer if we were united in our love of God and submission to his mission, but our churches will also be better with this focus. A church that focuses on a particular value above all else risks making that value more important than God himself.

Most of our faces are pleasant, even beautiful. Yet, if you look long and hard enough, almost all have flaws. Scrutiny of something basically beautiful only damages our honest assessment of it. We have bigger challenges to address than the insignificant flaws of the church. In all of our cities, there is real evil at work. There are women being bought and sold for money. Kids are physically, emotionally, and sexually abused. People are murdered, raped, and assaulted, and justice is denied. In all of our cities, people walk a dangerous line, with their hearts in rebellion to God and their lives rebelling to his loving rule. Still, some have not even heard about the blood spilled and love shown for them. This deserves our focus, not the church's minor flaws. The church is beautiful enough when it is submitted and loving the lost world. The church sincerely applying itself to worship, community, and mission is beautiful enough.

Does it have idiosyncrasies? Of course, and if we apply our best thinking and our limited energy to finding and exposing those flaws, there will be plenty to do. But this exertion is not only a wasteful use of our limited resources, it also starves the world from the goods of the kingdom with which we have been entrusted. I am not saying we should not critique the church— much of what I have written here is a critique—only that our critique should be confined to essential matters and should ultimately build up the church. "Do not let any unwholesome talk come out of your mouths, but only what is helpful for building others up according to their needs" are words for our time.[8]

UNDERGROUND people are not less critical than other Christians. We are just not making the minor flaws of other

Christians the focus of our critique and scrutiny. We reserve our prophetic fire for the devil and his schemes. We do not wrestle against flesh and blood; we wrestle against something more elusive and harder to find. These missionaries are too busy to write me an email about something I said that was inappropriate when they know my heart and see me as an ally in their struggle. They are too spent to comb through the sermons they hear or the songs they sing to find the bit they don't like, even though there are plenty of things they probably would change if it were up to them. We are trying to achieve unity, not uniformity. So instead of being critical, they are desperate to hear and hold in their hearts the bits of what I say that speak to them from God's Word—the bits that help them keep going and that remind them that there is hope yet for the people and places they labor. Most preachers I know would give anything for an audience like that. And, believe me, it is as good as it sounds.

Missionaries Aren't Looking for One Great Person to Lead Them

Scottish philosopher Thomas Carlye famously said, "The history of the world is but the biography of great men."[9] This "great man theory" persists today. We really believe that history is made by the actions and acumen of a few great men and women. We tend to recount history by referring to singular leaders. Writers like Herbert Spencer and the later deconstructionists like Derrida and Foucault would make the counter argument of "the great man myth." Essentially, men do not make history; these icons and icon-oclasts are merely products of their time. Their argument does not diminish great effort, innovation, or deeds; it only challenges this inaccurate way of remembering and retelling history. Men do not make history. History makes them.

Even Jesus, who was the one great man in history, blushed at being called "good" teacher.[10] Aside from the absurdity of such self-important versions of history, and the prohibition by Jesus (he said, "no one is good"), we still persist in wanting our church leaders to be exactly these kinds of great men in history. Deep down, so many young church leaders harbor a secret dream of being the next St. Francis, Martin Luther, John Wesley, or Mother Theresa. This desire is ultimately foiled by one inevitable reality: none of us are great men or women. God is the only one who is great. We are all, instead, mere servants—weak, flawed, and often ridiculous. At best, we are sorry for our flaws, submitted to God in our growth, and always listening and learning. The best kind of leader is the one who is self-aware, humble, and whose life is baptized in repentance. I hope to be that kind of leader.

My own sins, flaws, and errors in judgment have cost me throughout the years. If the UNDERGROUND were set up so that it needed a great man, I am sure it would have failed completely by now. This, too, has been a surprise—that we are together stronger than any one leader, and our collective righteousness is something that preserves us and allows us to give grace in weakness.

The biggest mistake I have ever made in ministry was growing into an emotionally dependent relationship with one of our ministry teammates, a woman who was not my wife. About five years before we started the UNDERGROUND, some fifteen years ago now, I was young and proud, and what doomed me in that relationship was the utter refusal to see my own weakness. I quickly realized it was unbalanced. My wife called me out on it. Those holding me accountable pressed into me about it. But I held onto the stubborn idea that I could manage it, that infidelity was beyond me. I idealized the relationship into some kind of crusade for equal discipleship between men and women. I even imagined that, although I felt some attraction to her, I should double down on the relationship in order to take away the stigma.

I kept trying to tell myself that Jesus was stronger and that we should not exclude people from leadership relationships just because we feel attracted to them. Maybe there is truth in that, but my undoing was my refusal to see my own frailty. The more dangerous the ground, the more entrenched I got. Knowing that we are weak is real strength. I have since learned that our greatest ideas can lead us into our deepest self-righteousness.

The relationship never materialized into an affair, but eventually we crossed physical lines, a single event that brought me as low as I have ever been. Still, those depths held incalculable grace. It was because of that indiscretion that I surrendered my life and leadership in a way I don't think I had before. I tried to save the friendship, but the results were mixed. We were all young leaders then with little experience in dealing with such things. We stumbled through it making mistakes in the process.

Everyone involved was miraculously gracious. My community walked with us. My wife never wavered in her commitment to me. The woman, my unhealthy friend and co-laborer, gave and received grace. But what I most needed, and what I have not let go of, is my own sense of frailty. It became a foundational value for the UNDERGROUND and a place of weakness from which I try to lead. The frailty still reverberates in me today. I am capable of great failure, I realized then, and I must always remember that. Every now and then, even all these years later, I experience some repercussions from that failure. While I know that I am forgiven, human beings have long memories, and sin has a way of finding new life and new reincarnations. So I find myself again receiving life from that cup of repentance. It is bitter, but its contents are life from God. If I am tempted again to walk in pride—to think any sin is beyond me—I remember this failing. And sometimes I cry.

I am happy for people to know about that failure, and others, because it forces them to consider my frailty and, I think, the inadequacy of all human leaders to ultimately save us. Most of our missionaries are not fazed by this revelation. There is no scandal here, partly because they know that they too have sin and that darkness is in their story, but also because they know that the whole enterprise of mission is predicated on grace.

We cannot be scandalized if we don't make idols out of our leaders. The scandal really is that God would use any of us. Ever. I suppose the other scandal is that we pretend our leaders are not flawed and inadequate people. To empower everyone to the possibility of leadership means we have to reconceive spiritual leadership as human or something human beings can do. Don't get me wrong. We need a high moral standard, and leaders who display a pattern of sin—evidenced by an unrepentant life—should not lead, but when we do fall short (which is not a question of if, but when), we have to carry the humility to grow and to learn from it. Repentance, humility, confession, and discipline will need a renaissance in the church if we are to become the kind of church leaders God wants us to be. We need more people doing it, which means we will need more discipline, more repentance, and more restoration.

There is a potent and caring accountability that we offer each other, because we believe that we are going to need it when we fail and because we know that there is always a road back for the repentant sinner. I have come to be delighted and surprised by just how important discipline, restoration, and grace is for a community like ours. It is part of the great leveling, reminding us that the church is not made up of great men or women, but ordinary people who worship a great God.

Mission, Like Leadership, Can Be Lonely

Finally, I have to say that from time to time I—and others in our network—have been surprised to feel a deep sense of loneliness in this work. At first, I wanted to be left alone. I wanted to be free from the scrutiny and the expectation that so many apostolic people feel. Yet, I was like the adolescent child that wants nothing so much as to be free from their parent's control, only to return to the existential need for their acceptance and approval. The down-side of being at the front of anything is that it can be very lonely. Even though we have each other, we still sometimes feel a craving for some kind of external validation. That is a vulnerable thing to share, but I share it because I know that the few who may be moved by our story, the brave ones who will give some of these ideas a real go, may also face that isolation.

When we started the UNDERGROUND, most of our people were in their twenties and thirties. Over the years, we have attracted some older leaders, even people over sixty, and it is hard to put into words the effect they have had on us. Wolfgang Simson wrote that a rebel is just a radical without his father's heart.[11] So it is that so many of our people feel that father or mother hunger.

Living as a missionary, I experience days when I work so hard and am so caught up in what I am doing that it doesn't occur to me to eat. It is not until food is offered that I realize just how hungry I am. When these older leaders—the mothers and fathers—have stepped into our relatively young community, we all have felt a collective hunger for their approval. Personally, I find myself responding to the requests of our older leaders with an almost irrational deference. All they have to do is drop their proverbial hat and I am there. I think this phenomenon is related to the loneliness we feel, because the presence of older believers is suddenly so important. We feel like we are being seen for the first time. Of course, we have each other, and we are not actually alone, but that feeling is still there. As a community in the world of church life and work, we are not sure anyone really understands or even cares.

There is brashness to our enterprise. We have stepped out on our own, as if to say, *We don't need your traditions or the affirmation of your system.* And yet, we do. We have a craving for someone to say, *You are doing a good job. We are proud of you.* While we get this directly from God and we offer it to each other, I think it is human nature to also crave that from older, established leaders. I have been surprised by just how important that approval is for us, especially since we had to be willing to forgo it for a time in order to do something new and brave. For those who will walk the road we have walked down, be prepared for loneliness, isolation, and even criticism. For those who are older, please don't underestimate the power of your words, affirmation, and approval. Be generous with it.

These are just some of the lessons we have learned, some of the ways that a community formed around mission surprised us. Some of these surprises are very good, but they are only possible because we have said "yes" to each other. The experiment was and remains predicated on our common commitment, not to a particular model, but to a set of values. It is this covenantal commitment that holds us together while also giving us the freedom to be creative. The power of that kind of covenant is one of our most important discoveries.

Chapter 8

OUR MANIFESTO

*Certain truths can be spoken only
from the well of exaggeration.*

BRENNAN MANNING

Words are what hold us together—a great idea is lost if it cannot be captured in words.

Conceiving of how things *might be* does no good if we cannot communicate that hope to other people. That is, a great *idea* ends with you if it cannot be captured in words. What is in a person's heart will have to be translated into speech or text in order for others to participate in that idea. All our hopes for the church are, by nature, collective hopes. They are not individualistic, and certainly they will not be accomplished alone. This puts tremendous weight on the mode and method of communication. That's what our Manifesto is all about.

There are two main conduits for meaning and communication within any given community: regular, everyday communication and formal, specialized communication. There is an obvious need in our enterprise for regular encouragement, inspiration, and memory—the first conduit. The missionaries in the UNDERGROUND face discouragement every day. Storm clouds are always forming, and there is an undeniable need for someone to remind them that what they do is worth it and that they should not give up. I cannot overstate the importance of this kind of constant encouragement. It is not the same as casting vision because we are not trying to steer these missionaries back to some master plan we have. Rather, it is more like the function of our memory. We have to regularly remind each other of the greatness of God, the desperation of the world, and the significance of what we do. Otherwise, the default settings kick in and we all drift back to comfort, security, and middle-class malaise.

While that kind of regular communication is important, the second conduit of communication—the formal manifesto type of communication—is more permanent. I think every community needs a rallying word, something that is unchanging and definitive like the Magna Carta, the United States Constitution, the Ninety-Five Theses, or even Jerry Maguire's mission statement.

Every community needs a galvanizing declaration that represents their collective heart and their intent in the world—bylaws for the soul. This might not seem to have anything to do with people, but it is the best version of shared meaning between people that fully manifests in written form. Part of the meaning comes from the fact that it's an outward expression of something shared by human hearts. Typically, this is expressed in mission, vision, and values. These three almost interchangeable constructs are the building blocks of businesses, social enterprises, and, yes, even churches. I would argue that families and even dyadic communities would often benefit from articulating their own manifestos.

This kind of communication is an attempt to say, *This is why we exist and this is why we matter.* Even though the use of these kinds of statements is everywhere, they can be heartless for groups and usually the work product of one or two people. I suggest that these statements only work if they are:

1. Prophetic: speaking uniquely to the needs and desperation of time and place

2. Aspirational: reaching for something beyond us—a hope and a dream of a better reality
3. Communal: expressing the anguish and aspiration of a critical mass of people

I believe the UNDERGROUND really started the day we finished our Manifesto, a document we initially just called "Our Core Values." At that moment, our hopes and dreams for a new kind of community saw the light of day. Thus, our mission began. For sure, we were groping toward it all before that moment, but the importance of this kind of document cannot be understated. Hence, I am devoting the rest of this chapter to its place and purpose in the life and legacy of our community. This is how the document begins:

> It is our belief that these are the values most needed to reshape the church, and if taken together and embraced, will revive the church and bring it into a new era of potency, resilience, and beauty. All that we imagine the church can be, it must aspire to again. Each is important, but our hope is for a gestalt effect in the hearing but, more importantly, also in the living of these values together.

1. JESUS

The way of Jesus is our way. Before and in all things, we value Jesus as the image of the invisible God. We long to worship Jesus by imitating his life and ministry. Both our theology and praxis is relentlessly Christological. He is our model, mentor, hero, mediator, savior, judge, king, and ruler of all. All of our values flow from what we understand about his character, concerns, and the practices of his ministry. (Matthew 28:19, John 1:3, John 13:15, John 14:6, John 17:18, Romans 5:10, Ephesians 1:22–23, Philippians 2:5, Colossians 1:15–20, Colossians 2:9, Colossians 3:17, Hebrews 1:3, Hebrews 12:2, [MODEL] Ephesians

5:1–2, [MENTOR] John 13:14–15, Acts 26:16, [HERO] Romans 1:4, [MEDIATOR] 1 Timothy 2:5, Hebrews 7:25, [SAVIOR] Acts 4:12, Titus 3:6, [JUDGE] Romans 2:16, John 9:39, 2 Timothy 4:1, [KING] Revelation 1:5, Revelation 19:16, [RULER OF ALL] Colossians 1:18, Revelation 17:14).[1]

This articulation of our convictions provides the boundaries for our self-definition; it is the glue that holds us together through disagreements; it calls us forward in hope; and it gives us a standard by which to measure ourselves.

The Boundaries of Defining Ourselves

Every living thing on earth has a body, that is, physical dimensions existing and interacting with the world. We can think about the embodiment of organizations and churches in the same way. The New Testament writers want us to understand the church as the body of Jesus. Like physical bodies, the shape and form of the church can take on thousands of valid expressions. At the UNDERGROUND, we have embraced that flexibility and diversity. Almost any form of church can join our network. Yet, even though we are inclusive of various types of bodies, we too need to understand and articulate our boundaries. Like other inclusive organizations, we have the obligation to define ourselves by asking, *What does it mean to belong to this body?*

Some Christian communities define themselves by certain ecclesial traditions with a focus on church practices. We might say, as a way of declaring our loyalty to a certain church tradition, "I go to that church." Other communities are more defined by doctrine, allowing for a wide variety of ecclesial practices. They answer the question, "What does it mean to belong to this body?" more doctrinally by saying, "I am Reformed" or "I am Catholic." These statements, however, may or may not have anything to do with how often you actually attend either kind of church. Still others define their connection to a church through vision. That is, they buy into the vision of a particular church. The vision might be for kids or for disciple-making or for racial reconciliation. Every group needs to define what it means or what it takes to be a part of it, and conversely, what it would not mean to be a part of it. That is where a church's manifesto or beliefs statement comes into play.

Recently, an article run by *Time Magazine* on InterVarsity Christian Fellowship USA exposed an internal document outlining their position on human sexuality and, in particular, their long-held position that same sex relationships are outside the bounds of scriptural holiness. Failure to hold this position as a staff member, the article said, would result in termination. The article created a stir, which elicited strong criticism from all kinds of Christians.

Part of what I considered unfair about the article was the implication that this was somehow a new position. In fact, InterVarsity has held this orthodox Christian position for its entire seventy-five-year organizational history. Yet, because of the growing uncertainty around the issue, they entered into a three-year-long process to explore the topic honestly with people who held differing positions. Ultimately, the process concluded with a reaffirmation of their long-held belief and the continuation of their expectation that staff members agree with their major theological convictions, including this one. Further, they encouraged all staff supervisors to work with dissenting staff in a way that was thoughtful and honorable. There was no scandal in the end, but InterVarsity was being punished in the court of public perception for doing what every healthy organization must do to survive—clarify its identity.

It may be that this particular issue was not central enough to lose staff over, or some might argue that the historic theological position they held was wrong. Still, do they not have the right of self-definition? Also, why would anyone argue that someone who held a profoundly contrary position, for what both parties consider to be an essential issue, should be allowed or expected to remain an employee of the organization?

As I mentioned above, networks are becoming increasingly popular, and I believe they will continue to emerge. Networks are coming up alongside, apart from, or even separate from denominations. The challenge of this new form of church organization for today, though, is a clearly defined identity. Networks start up easily enough, usually galvanized by one or two issues, but over time, some practices and beliefs remain undefined, which can become a kind of irritant to belonging. When people begin to realize that not everyone in the network holds certain essential beliefs and behavioral standards, there is dissonance and eventually dissent. What started from a desire to simplify a particular issue and unify becomes the very seedbed of dissension.

How then can we embrace the contextually verdant model of network without creating more division in the future? Clearly defined values, I believe, are the key. If we create clarity on the core values of our networks and these values are both nonnegotiable (we cannot live without them) and also a little bit beyond our current practice (we admit we don't all fully live them), we create a unity that can only come from the pursuit of a common goal.

Belonging in the UNDERGROUND is not based on participation (you do not have to come to things); it is not based on one person's vision (we are a multiplicity of visions); and it is not based on one theological tradition (there is room for all Orthodox Christian streams). It is based on a shared set of aspirational values and a covenant to try to keep them. These values are an attempt to describe the nonnegotiables for us, what it means to be in partnership with us in the mission of God. As open as it is, it is still totally limited.

Because it is only eighteen values, the Manifesto not only gives us what we need people to believe, but also, in turn, what we do not need them to believe. We don't have a manifesto of *beliefs* (in the traditional sense); we have a *values* manifesto—and the distinction here is important. Let me explain the difference by way of example.

We have wrestled with the question of women in roles of leadership within the church (a theological belief). This is not because we as individuals or microchurches are unclear on it (I am personally a strong proponent of women in every leadership role in the church), but because we had to deal with more important issues of missional exclusion. I believe one thing, but am I willing to exclude other leaders who hold a different view, particularly if that view is directed from a sincere reading of Scripture? We are on mission, and our values, not our particular beliefs about controversial topics, make us a group.

I know plenty of complementarian leaders, those who believe in limited leadership roles for women, who have agonized over the position and have come to it from their attempt to faithfully understand and live the Word of God. If those people want to serve the homeless in our city, for example, are we not going to support them and offer them fellowship in the pursuit of that mission? I want the homeless to become disciples. I can live with the dissonance on that one issue if they will lay down their lives for the people who need the good news of the kingdom. Perhaps they will overlook my more liberal point of view for the same reason.

The solution to that issue for us is expressed in our eighteenth value, empowerment. In it, we summarize how empowerment is nonnegotiable for our community. If God calls someone, we do not block them from that call; instead, we nurture their call. If a group of men and women hold a complementarian view together and the women in that community do not feel in any way disempowered by that, then we can respect that difference. As long as they are pursuing mission (the good news of the kingdom given to this poor and broken world), then they are family. The deeper value for us, then, and the way we define ourselves, is calling. If you are called, you are welcomed in.

Articulating Our Aspirations

There is a difference between doctrine and values. Doctrine is what we know to be true about God. Values are what should therefore be true about us. God is compassionate—that is a matter of doctrine. It is what we can see, read, and know about God. The companion value, then, is derivative; it comes from that truth about God. We ought to be compassionate because he is. He shows mercy and generosity to those who suffer, who are in need, and to those who have been systematically excluded. Agreeing on doctrine alone will not bring missional unity because it does not explicitly apply to us.

It is my opinion that human community (in all its forms) is doomed until it applies theology to relationships. It is this all-important transition from what we know about God to how we should then live (and relate to each other) that is so critical to our flourishing together. Every church will need to agree (at least in essentials) on their doctrine, but it is really the values that we share, and more to the point, the values we want to live that hold us together in witness to the power and beauty of the kingdom.

Most people understand the need for unifying statements. They know that we need to agree to terms before we can work together. But if those terms are usually only doctrinal, we have not agreed on the *way* we will work together. We have agreed on who we believe God to be and maybe even who we believe the church is supposed to be, but our values determine how we will express that in the small space between you and me. To take that distinction a step further, we wrote values that were not just what we already do or think, but what we hope to do and think. Perhaps one of the most important characteristics of our Manifesto is that it is aspirational.

Each value is not a self-referential mirror. We were not necessarily trying to catalog what we already do, but what we dream of doing. The document is beyond us. It calls to us, and it unifies us, not just in our ascension to the truth of it, but in the journey to do it. This kind of aspirational expression of our doctrine-become-values is deeply humbling and resists the always-present danger of self-righteousness. The experience of reading our Manifesto (at least for me) is at once an experience of resonance as well as inadequacy. This is exactly the kind of unifying document we need. It is prophetic in its voice, and it speaks directly to us.

A doctrinal statement might be something that can be pulled together in a few days, simply by reading others and deciding the bits that you agree with most. But the type of values statement like I am talking about is generative, and it should take months of listening and conversation to create it.

Listening First

In the very early days of the UNDERGROUND, before we had become anything concrete as a group, we gathered every other week to uncover our convictions. We alternated our listening. One week, we would listen to each other by brainstorming, and the next, we would listen to God through prayer. The prayer sessions gave us a sense of what we thought God was asking from us and from the church in our city. The brainstorm sessions gave us a chance to talk through our frustrations with the status quo in the church as we had experienced it. We took note of all those ideas, as well as the emotion behind them. The smaller team then took those notes to the Philippines with us to further debate and distill our thoughts, until finally, I shut myself away to write the first draft of the Manifesto. It took us months and many hours of deliberation to create it. It is not perfect, but it is a document that is truly ours. For me, it is timeless and universal (the goal is not to create a document that only applies to you, but can apply to anyone). Yet, it is uniquely an expression of our hearts and our understanding of God and his call to his people.

I think it was the Reformed Theological Seminary professor Richard Pratt who first put me on to three legs of Christian righteousness. Think of a three-legged stool, it will not hold weight without all three. Orthodoxy is only one leg of the stool (correct teaching), but the others—orthopraxy (correct action) and orthopathos (correct emotion)—are similarly nonnegotiable. It is not hard to see how certain traditions have leaned on one over another. While the reformers continue to fight for orthodoxy, the Catholics hold up orthopraxy, and the Pentecostals cry out for orthopathos. We all pine for a community that will offer us hope for the full righteousness of God. Its value statements, like our Manifesto, demand all three from the life of the believer and the collective work of the community. Authentic articulation of those three convictions is not something you can uncover in a weekend. I would encourage every new community to go through the process of listening to God and to each other and ironing out your values.

When a new leader or ministry wants to become a part of the UNDERGROUND, we always point them to the Manifesto. It is our filter, and we always say the same thing: we don't just want you to agree with it, but to agree to living it. We also don't want anyone to contort their convictions to fit. When you read it, you either think, *This is exactly how I feel (already),* or you don't. Those who do not agree with our values don't have to conform, but then they are not a part of the UNDERGROUND, and we gladly release them to find a more fitting group. It's better that they find out sooner than later. No negotiating, no qualifying, no exceptions. In our open-handed, trusting environment, this initial moment of rigidity is everything. We can be open later if we are closed here.

We can be free, trusting, and empowering later because we hold to this standard of the heart.

Do people sometimes lie about their love for the Manifesto in order to get free services? Sure. Dishonesty is always a risk, but it happens a lot less than you might imagine. Most of the time people are moved by it. They may not have been able to put all of their own aspirations into words the same way we have, but when they read it, they know we are already a part of the same tribe (or not). Because these kinds of leaders are so hungry to belong and to find a community that gets them, this kind of experience is just what they need. It is a filter for us, but it is equally a filter for them. We are wondering if they carry our values, but they are wondering the same thing about us. The Manifesto, then, is the pitch we strike, one with which everyone must be in tune.

The Glue That Binds Us: Values, Not Vision

Most of us would agree that values and value statements are important, even crucial, in the life of any enterprise. But a part of what makes our reliance on the Manifesto unique is its relationship (or lack of relationship) to the idea of vision. I have written elsewhere about my love-hate relationship with the leadership concept of vision. It is hard to find a more celebrated tactic for leaders in the last forty years. The key to great leadership seems to always be communicating vision. Theorists like John Kotter have argued that you cannot undercommunicate vision. Take whatever vision casting you naturally do, and multiply it 1,000 times.[2]

This overstatement is meant to echo the almost religious fervor with which leaders have laid claim to a business notion that was once relegated to the realm of fairy tales and theophany. Even 100 years ago, if someone said they had a vision, they would have been making a claim to something supernatural. What, after all, is a vision? Prophets and seers have visions; vision is a religious idea, so we should go to religion, not business, to understand how to communicate it.

Those who follow visionaries and their visions, those would-be adherents, must also be believers. These believers have to trust that the dream or vision was given to the seer as a divine gift. The implication is that a leader's followers (whether they believe in a God or not) must attribute godlike gifts to the leader they follow. Entire faith traditions are based on one person's visionary revelations (e.g., Islam and Mormonism). They must believe that the vision of the future they have seen is both desirable and possible. This is the dangerous thing—that the leader who has received the vision is the one to lead his people there. The leader then must "cast" this vision to their audience, presumably in order to awaken the loyalty and labor of the listener.

The problem with this notion of visionary leadership in the church is not that we can't believe in divine vision. We should believe in divine vision. The problem is that this definition of vision is *too narrow*. We are confusing vision with strategy. It is this kind of vision that always carries with it a corresponding demand for alignment. To compound the problem, in the church, the bearer of the vision is claiming more than just a good idea or a possible direction in which to go, they are offering God's actual plan. A person who has a genuine vision from God should, in my view, not care all that much about having control over how it comes to pass. They might not even necessarily believe that they were essential to its accomplishment. What if, for instance, in the deep place of prayer, I have a vision of a city without orphans. It's a beautiful and maybe even God-inspired vision. Why would I then need to control how that comes to pass? Maybe there is a revival of families, and kids are just no longer abandoned. Maybe extended families just start caring for every kid. Or maybe there is a wave of compassion that comes over the city, swelling the ranks of foster and adoptive parents. Having that vision would not mean anything about my leadership or control over that process. I would just want to see it happen.

The way church leaders currently handle vision can sometimes be unhealthy and at times even dangerous. When the church leader has a vision, it usually means that all those who would walk under that leader are asked to "get on board" with the vision of the church. Practically then, this too often means restricting the work and investment of the people in the church to the programs and mission of the church, and nothing else. Leaders who have taken this mandate to heart have possibly fallen victim to an inferior approach to leadership. Where is this mandate in the Bible?

I think this kind of leadership is cast from the Old Testament archetype of Moses, which does not reflect the New Testament revolution in leadership that Jesus ushered in. We see the leader as God's singular mediator, the consolidation of his friendship and will to lead a deaf and rebellious people. Moses goes up the mountain (that none of the common people can even touch or they will die) and talks to the God that is beyond their reach. When he comes down from the mountain of prayer, he is enraptured with both the glory and the words of God. He is glowing, for goodness' sake. Moses's vision was about what kind of people they were called to be as described by God in his Law. This archetype is consistent with the image of a visionary leader. The visionary leader comprehends and then delivers the vision, and the rest of us need only to follow it. Their work is receiving the vision, and our work is aligning with it.

But is this appropriate for the church today in exactly this way? What about the priesthood of all believers? We need to reckon with how the cross has changed forever the dynamics of a leader's relationship with their people. First, as I have already argued, their leadership must be governed by servanthood. The visionary leader can be tempted to make each person a servant to their vision, yet the church already has a leader: Jesus. He is the head of the church. He is the firstborn from among the dead. He is the first and the last. He is the author and the perfecter of our faith. He is the head of his church. Not us.

The day of Pentecost is especially relevant for the major shift that has occurred for the people of God. We no longer need an intermediary because "we all, who with unveiled faces contemplate the Lord's glory . . . which comes from the Lord, who is the Spirit."[3] Our work as under-shepherds and servant leaders then is not to tell people what the vision of God is for them, but to show them the way up the mountain. It is not to be Moses for them, but to show them that because of Jesus we can all have the kind of intimate friendship with God that Moses enjoyed. We are the first to go and the first to teach others where to go. The rabbis tell us that the Torah (Law) was given on a very specific day: the feast of Shavuot. That might not register until we call it by its more familiar New Testament name, the day of Pentecost. God provided his Spirit on the anniversary of the day he provided his Law. The Spirit was poured out—not upon one believer—but upon all believers. We all drink of the same Spirit. "Your young men will see visions, your old men will dream dreams."[4]

We need visions, and we need dreams. We need to return to a biblical conception of these beautiful ideas. The idea of vision was ours before it was a business concept, and it should still be in use by our prophets and our dreamers. Vision is our word because we all need supernatural sight from God, for his kingdom and for the future he imagines for us. It is a religious word (and it should be the purview of the church), but for many leaders, it has been coopted by the business world and then sold back to them, twisted and vacant of its true meaning. Visions should be offered (like all prophecy) as edification of the people and as alignment to God himself, and while there can be times that we also hear a word of alignment for our people, we ought to handle that with extreme care and humility. We have to call people ultimately to the values of the kingdom lived in their lives and contexts. Sometimes that will mean we are drawing them in to something we have discerned, but more often than not (especially for a leader who has oversight of other leaders), we need to keep an open hand, urging our people to listen to the voice and vision of God for their own life and ministry. I still think we can experience strong alignment in teams, even through the vehicle of vision, but because each person has had the same vision, not necessarily because I have convinced them to see mine. I am arguing that the best way to love and lead our people is not to call them to our vision, but to call them to the values of the kingdom and release them to see a vision for how that looks in their own life.

The church should not be a place where one visionary leader acts as the single mediator between the common people and God. The church should be a place where everyone can express a vision or a dream. The responsibility of ecclesial leadership is to create environments where dreams and visions are commonplace and, even more to the point, where people who get a vision from God can actually pursue it without being ostracized as someone who is not "on board" with the pastor's vision.

I know that to disparage the sacredness of the ubiquitous vision statement will be met with some disagreement. And honestly, I could be wrong about all this. But I also want to offer a working alternative that is a faithful reflection of our community. This is how we have come to work together. We have discovered that one vision statement used as a unifier is inferior to a series of values. Our Manifesto paints a picture. It is a dream and, in a very real sense, serves as the "vision statement" for our community. It has allowed for a thousand other more specific visions and dreams of the kingdom coming. Still, instead of one reductionist vision statement, we express the values that we believe should hold us together or that will bear witness to the world we believe is possible. The Manifesto, then, is an alternative. We are saying new church communities need value statements over vision statements, just as they need to embrace servant structures over controlling ones. The glue that will hold a network of autonomous, empowered missionaries together will be a standard of values, not visionary mandates. The distinction might be subtle, but it is everything to us. Our microchurch leaders do not want to be told what to do, but they do want to be held accountable to how they do it.

The Sum of Our Parts

A few years back, I struck up a friendship with a guy who was on staff at a megachurch. He was intrigued and inspired by our way of life and of mission. With the encouragement of his senior pastor, he came and spent a few days with us to try and take some ideas back to their team. While he was with us, we showed him a little of the behind-the-curtain work, including our Manifesto. I soon lost touch with him, until someone called me, out of the blue, to ask if I knew that a big church in a certain city was using parts of our Manifesto. I didn't immediately make the connection, but I eventually realized how they had come to start using so many of our values (verbatim). At first, I was encouraged. *Good,* I thought, *the more people committing to these ideas, the better.*

However, I came to really struggle with the kind of counter-mandate I read in their version. It was not the use of our words that troubled me; it is what they left out. For instance, they chose to include our value statement about serving the lost, but not the poor. What does an omission like that say? If you knew the theology behind these values, you would know that my understanding of lostness (unbelief) is actually a derivative of poverty. Poverty is the more important biblical concept. To exclude the poor is not only to fail a thousand biblical mandates, it is also to misunderstand evangelism.

Equally painful was the realization that they had excluded our value for every culture and multiethnicity. No doubt, they left these out because these two do not (I am assuming) represent the life and practice of their church. Maybe they made those editorial changes not because they disagree with them, but because they wanted to maintain a sense of integrity. Yet, the fact that they are a predominantly white, middle-class church is precisely why they need to keep those values. They may (to the mind of God) actually be the most important ones for them.

This church kept other values, but materially changed them. Simplicity, for instance, which in our rendition is about the prophetic call to resist the demonic powers of greed and materialism so rampant and unchecked in our culture, got a makeover. They, like others who talk about simplicity, have twisted it to mean something aesthetic, as if simplicity is more about getting rid of clutter or tidying up—simplicity as the feng shui of church. The value of decluttering is *not* the same as the value of deaccumulation. Simplicity, as we have understood it, is something much more demanding and prophetic. Again, it seems like this version of our ideas was sanitized to support what they are already doing or believing. Somehow, their statements seemed to have lost their teeth. For this reason, I recommend coming up with your own values from scratch, not starting with someone else's manifesto.

Maybe it is okay for them to shape a set of values that reflect their own culture and sensibilities. As I have already argued, they should be empowered to do that. I am not judging them for that; I am reflecting on the experience of seeing the Manifesto taken apart and what the experience made me realize. I can see now how important each value was to me and that, taken together, they represent something else entirely. There is a gestalt quality to the Manifesto. I realize that it is not just that each value is important to us, but that they need to be lived in concert with each other. For instance, the pursuit of the value for "each other" without the equally important values of mission in "the lost" and "the poor" could actually become unhealthy.

This year, for the first time in our lives, one of my adult kids, Eve, was not able to come to Thanksgiving. For the first time, too, I felt a corresponding emptiness at her absence. My wife and six children make up the whole of my nuclear family. They are each unique and each beloved. It begs the question, *Is it a family gathering if the whole family isn't together?* It does not mean that I didn't treasure the time with my other children this Thanksgiving, but the presence of some does not negate the absence of others. In some deep, existential way, I sensed that void. There is a space in our family that only Eve can fill, and when she is not there, we are not whole.

I don't mean to be melodramatic, but I feel the same way about the values in our Manifesto. There is not one that I consider a cousin or a distant relative. There are plenty of biblical values that are dear to us, but that did not make this list in the first place. It does not express everything in the world that is important to us, but these are the essentials. They make up the nuclear family of our ideas, a composition of the nonnegotiables that unify us as a missional family. Therefore, we are not just asking people to agree with each of them, but to agree with the collection itself. Each one is a valid and important value, but taken together, they are the Manifesto of our community.

An Audit of Our Hearts

At the end of every year since we started, I retreat with the senior leaders of our movement to assess ourselves in light of the Manifesto. It is not a time for metrics or cold analysis, but rather a time of prayer, dreaming, repentance, and hope. We stand naked before the promises we have made to God, and our Manifesto is there to measure us. We ask ourselves what values are drifting from our hearts. It is first a time of reflecting on our own lives and ministries and then (as best we perceive it) on the life and ministry of our movement. It is not enough to write a document like this. It has to be stewarded in the life of our community. Perhaps it is closer to the monastic concept of a "Rule of Life," providing us with both cooperate identity and a communal goal. It has to be front and center in our initial conversations with new leaders. It is the first word that brings us together, and it is the last word in our assessment of our growth, development, and witness in the world. It is not that these words replace the Bible. Scripture is still our own rule for life and faith, but that vast sea is summarized in this document, as a word from God for us, in our time. The Bible is itself one of these values, so all that it teaches is therefore also contained in the Manifesto. Still, this is our attempt to say what we think the church should care about and look like. It is our intimacy with the ideas and their wording that becomes invaluable to our mission, to our identity, and to our power as a community.

WINDOW 2

It's 10:00 a.m. on Wednesday morning, and I can hear the conference room next to my office filling up. Along with our young movement, our leadership team has grown too. All the seats are taken now, and our long conference table is buzzing as jokes are made, stories are swapped, and phones are checked. I am the last to arrive, with a drink in one hand and a book of prayers by Walter Brueggemann in the other. We start in our usual way: department heads and key staff, which are more than twelve now, each pray, offering a single sentence. We take a deep breath after each line is offered and received. I finish with a prayer from Brueggemann's book:

> We imagine ourselves called by you . . .
> Yet a strange lot:
>> called but cowardly,
>> obedient but self-indulgent,
>> devoted to you, but otherwise preoccupied.
> In our strange mix an answering and refusing,
> We give thanks for your call.
> We pray this day,
>> for ourselves, fresh vision;
>> for our friends, great courage,
>> for those who search for you
>>> in places more dangerous than ours,
>>> deep freedom.

As we seek to answer your call, may we be haunted
by your large purposes,
We pray in the name of the utterly called Jesus.
　　Amen.[1]

I brush away a tear. What we do is important, and we all know it. But more than that, the privilege of having the chance to do this as our work has never worn off. I ask if there is anything to add to the agenda, and a few people offer pressing issues. More jokes are made. (We probably laugh as much as we work.) I look over at Leann, because I already know we have some microchurch applications (we call them "start something forms"), and she takes it from there. These are our favorite moments at staff meetings.

She tells us we have three new submissions, so we all check our team communications app feed as she tells us which one to look at first. The first one is a no brainer: we know the leaders, and they want to start a recording studio and label for homeless musicians. We know them from their work in another microchurch. For years, they have run an open mic event for the street community, so we know that many of their connections are musically talented. We read through their idea. I see that they have agreed to the Manifesto, and I scan ahead to the all-important question, *How will you incorporate worship, community, and mission into your idea?* I love their answer. I look up and see everyone nodding as they read.

"Seems great to me," I say. "Any objections?"

"Nope."

"None."

"No way."

"This is a great idea."

"Isn't it?" I grin.

Green light. Everyone puts "the people's music" into their task list. The next step for this new microchurch is that its leaders will get six emails, one of which welcomes them to the network and an invitation to an orientation meeting where one of our staff will walk them through all our key policies and some of the key opportunities they might want to take advantage of right away. They will also get an email from each department head, all of whom will now work with these leaders to get them what they need to be successful. This new microchurch just hit the jackpot.

I jump up. In the top right corner of our giant whiteboard is a number, the number of microchurches we have given a green light to so far this year. I wipe off "37" and put "38" in its place.

"Okay, what's next?" I clap my hands.

Start something form #2. "This one is not so straightforward," Leann says. The idea of their mission is harder to understand, we start to realize. Only one of us has met the leader who submitted it. Plus, there are clear problems with our Manifesto—their idea is all about serving Christians. There is nothing about mission to the lost or the poor, nothing expanding the kingdom to new territory, just a ministry idea for Christians. And it looks like they might not have many of those to start with. I look at the question about their team—*Who is currently on your team?* They have listed only their spouses.

We can't say yes to this one. Their values do not align with our Manifesto.

But that's not the end of it, of course. Keisha says she

knows who the leader is (and has talked to her once or twice).

"I like her," she says. "I think there is a mission in here; they just need help to find it."

"You willing to do the follow-up?"

"Happy to," she says.

Anthony puts that one on a different list. We will see how that meeting goes. Keisha will do some discipleship and see if there is not a dream for reaching the nonbelieving world somewhere in their hearts. If there is, she will draw it out. If not, that's okay too; we will wish them well, but it's not within our mission.

"Okay, last one then." We read on.

This one carries some debate. The idea has an element involving money, which makes some of the team uncomfortable. But it is missional. We just aren't so sure about the leaders. We go back and forth. I want to green light it, but enough of the team has reservations, so I give it to Jeremy. He is one of our most accomplished leaders, an expert in starting microchurches and gifted with discernment. I know if anyone can get this team moving in the right direction, it is Jeremy.

"Will you follow up this one?"

"Sure," he says.

"Can we look at it again next week?" I say.

Everyone agrees, because we all want to say yes.

Most weeks are like that—a mix. Yet, sometimes, it is all yeses, and sometimes, there is only one submission. If we go more than a week without one, we stop and pray or I press the team for the leads they are currently chasing. We plant microchurches, we support them, and we cheer for them. We live and die with them. This is what we do.

We go on to talk about an UNDERGROUND event we are planning and a few problems we are encountering. We also deal with some team dynamic struggles, but through it all, I can see that number in my peripheral sight. One more—one more team empowered, one more creative idea blessed, one more unreached group of people touched, discipled, and loved.

I purse my lips, thinking about our enemy and those principalities, those dark powers enslaving our city, distracting our people from Jesus and his gospel, his grace, his justice. I think about the devil. One more shot to his mouth, one more blow, one more tear in the veil that shrouds our city in darkness, and one more church. Take that!

We wrap up. We take our stand.

We get back to work.

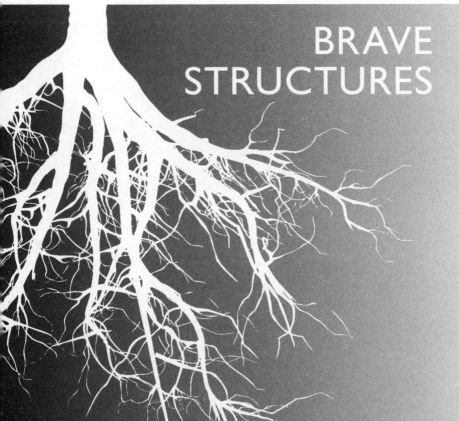

Part 3

BRAVE
STRUCTURES

Chapter 9

LEADERSHIP

*The little people must be sacred to the big
ones, and it is from the rights of the weak
that the duty of the strong is comprised.*

VICTOR HUGO

When I grew up in Florida, football was a big part of our world. We watched it some, but mostly we played the game. Every day in the summer, and most days during the school year, we played two-on-two in the street, with the gutters as the out-of-bounds limits. The street meant two-hand touch, but the real games were on Fridays after school. I lived for those games. We counted the minutes until the bell rang so we could get home, change our clothes, and meet at the park near my house. That game became legendary. We would long remember and mythologize neighborhood heroes and their exploits.

Friday games, of course, were tackle—no pads, no referees, just fierce play. Bigger kids and kids from other schools and neighborhoods would hear about it and come to play. We were proud of that game. Someone always got injured, which was also a part of the legendary stories we would tell. I once saw a guy break his arm so badly that he left the field with the bone sticking out. I can honestly say these games were some of the happiest times of my childhood, and that is only true because no matter how many people came, everyone got to play. If you showed up, you played.

I played in that game all through middle school and high school. Some of us also tried to play organized high school ball, but I can say that those games didn't bring me half the joy. In organized ball, only a few of the people on our team got to play. Many of us would just stand on the sidelines and watch. We were dressed; we had prepared; we wanted to play; but we never got in the game.

But those organized games had spectators—so many spectators. The whole thing really was a spectacle. I know that is what some players loved most about it, but it didn't mean much to me because I never got in the game.

In my, albeit limited, experience, North American churches are built like those organized football games. A few play for the spectators; a few sit on the sidelines hoping to play; and the rest, the vast majority, just watch. How tragic. It's tragic because the world is waiting for the church, this sleeping giant, to awaken to its abundance of gifts, energy, resources, and networks. It's tragic for the lost to wait in vain for someone to bring the gospel to where they are. It's tragic for the King of the kingdom, who has given his authority to us all, to watch his unopened gift lie dormant. And it is tragic for us, because the real joy is not in the game where everyone is watching, but in the game where everyone plays.

We became neighborhood legends in that Friday game, and that was more than enough for us. Not everyone can be the senior pastor of a massive church, but everyone can play a major role in a small church. I was never the best player, but I made some epic plays. I was not the best tackler, but I laid some guys out, reveling in it for days.

We forget that when everyone plays, it is not just mission that is multiplied, but the joy is also multiplied, because there is no greater joy in this life than to be used by God in the work of redemption. To play before a cheering throng might feel better, but only better for a select few. Maybe this is why Martin Luther imagined the priesthood of all the believers and why the Protestant project is built upon this idea. We all can play for the glory of Jesus, the multiplication of the church, and the fullest possibility of joy.

As I have already argued, a feature of both the New Testament vision for the church and this new creator economy in which we find ourselves is presuming abundance instead of scarcity. We have to make this move toward a mindset of abundance by seeing that the real strength and resource of the church is its people, not its buildings or its programs. We are rich with people, who are in turn rich with gifts, passion, networks, and ideas. This is our place of abundance. Buildings, money, and clergy are harder to find.

If we plant churches based on buildings (scarcity), money (scarcity), professional clergy (scarcity), or complicated work (scarcity), where is the abundance? But if we look at the people of God as seeds for the kingdom, each one representing the birth of not just an expression of the church, but something transformative and life giving to them and the world around them, then we are suddenly flush with hope. It is ordinary people who hold the key to the coming kingdom, because it is ordinary people who are its best and truest witnesses.

If we want only the A-game players on the field, the rest of us watching, then we can be fine with our current approach. If, however, we want to see the church living unbridled with a wild fire in our bones, then we will have to conceive of a game where everyone plays and where there is abundance—abundance of creativity, of people, and ultimately of joy. One of the most important implications of the UNDERGROUND experiment is that we have discovered a form of church where everyone plays. Even I am left wondering, *How did we do that? How did we get everyone to play, or perhaps, what must have come first, for these individuals to see themselves as players?* This is especially challenging, I've found, when the game involves pain.

Getting Mad

Somewhere in history, church became a place, a destination, and an event. That's why we *go to* church. But this isn't at all what Jesus had in mind when he first referred to his people as church. "You are Peter," he told Simon, the willful and bold disciple, "and on this rock I will build my church, and the gates of Hades will not overcome it."[1] The church, then, is something Jesus is building— something he builds through and on his people. It is something that is (at least in his vision for it) bombarding the gates of hell. The church is supposed to be people who are proactively engaging and impeding the prison of hell. Of course, that has evangelistic implications, but it also has psychological and sociological implications. To be the church, we are supposed to be mobilizing disciples of Jesus to fight something.

In the UNDERGROUND, when we help people find their personal calling, one of the six factors we consider is what's called our "emotional inventory." A big part of how we take that emotional inventory is by uncovering what makes a person genuinely angry. That is to say, we want to know what evil or wrong in the world makes a person genuinely mad. You might think that every evil would make us equally mad, but that is not the case. There are some things toward which we are either apathetic or by which we are only mildly bothered. There are some evils, however, that the Spirit of God uses to break through our apathy, and we are truly moved every time we encounter them, for whatever reason. While it is not always righteous, I am convinced that this anger is often a marker that points to something about who we are and where God is calling us.

Picking a Fight

When we talk about the UNDERGROUND's purpose internally, we think of four commitments, four things we want to do:

1. Help people surrender their whole lives to Jesus as Lord,
2. Help people find their calling,
3. Connect people to a community who share that calling, and
4. Engage evil in all its forms with prayerful action.

If you think of these as linear, which they often are, then the endgame is communities of disciples who fight against evil. That might be a negative way of putting it, but this idea has resonated with many of us. That's why I share it with you.

Perhaps one of the real failings of the church (the assembly of God's people) in our time is that we have not recognized that we are in a fight. But we are very much in a fight. While I am reluctant to overuse the metaphor of the soldier or the people of God as combatants, it is, in fact, a biblical image.[2] We are, at least in part, supposed to understand that our lives together are meant to contend for something. In the letters to the churches in Revelation, Jesus commends his people who have persevered to the end as those who have *overcome*. That word, *nikaō/overcome*, which could also be rendered *conqueror* or *victorious*, is used in every commendation to the churches in Revelation 2 and 3. Jesus means to remind his people that we are in a battle, a struggle that is very old and very important.

Ultimately, this is Jesus's fight. However, this cosmic contest between good and evil, light and darkness, truth and lies, love and hatred is our fight too. So much of the language of Revelation is meant to illuminate this epic struggle in which we are all engaged. The wrath, the judgment, and the whole drama really unfolds as the end of that struggle and as a final blow to everything that is not the kingdom. When Jesus finally appears, resplendent and indomitable, it is as a rider on a white horse, with a sword on his side and an army at his back.[3]

We must remember our call in terms of these breathtaking images. We are not just trying to help one person; that victory is merely a microcosm of the grand struggle for which God has been bending history since the beginning of time. Mission is not only good deeds, nor is it merely truth telling. It is good deeds in protest and resistance to sin and evil deeds. It is truth in defiance to lies, and it is freedom in enmity with captivity. "So God, the creator and healer of all," John Cassian wrote, "has been careful to heal opposites with opposites . . ."[4] We preach Jesus because the world loves idols. We break chains because the empire of Babylon keeps binding us.

I am not a triumphalist by nature, but how can we not be moved by these ideas? How can we fail to reframe our work as the church in the light of this eschatological reality? Seeing the church merely as a sheep pen, as a place for quiet contemplation, for potluck dinners, and for vacation Bible schools is not only inadequate, it is potentially dangerous. It can be dangerous because it so easily pacifies us into complacent disengagement. While this Norman Rockwell version of the church might be pleasant enough, even seeming innocuous, we have to ask what is not being done because we chose it. If I am right and the church is supposed to be a force to be reckoned with and a threat to evil everywhere, then a passive church is tantamount to treason. We are idle in a time of war. We are deserters.

The Whole Mission

When Jesus called and sent his followers into the world, he gave them three assignments: community, worship, and mission. All three of these still apply. We are called to proclaim the good news of the kingdom of God, heal the sick, and cast out demons.[5] These actions represent archetypes for mission and the work of the church. We preach the truth of the gospel; we work against sickness, death, and decay; and we oppose demonic forces in all their forms.

Preaching is still regarded by the church today as part of its core work; less so, care for the sick and the physically needy; least of all, the mandate to confront the demonic. With regard to confronting the demonic, this is more than just spiritual warfare, which is real and important. But to make it all about individual demons or internal turmoil is to completely underestimate the demonic. The demonic can also be at work in systems—anywhere power is wielded. We must discern and then resist these evil powers.

This is all to say that we have to get into the fight against demonic forces. We must find a fray, a breach, a gap in which to stand. In my experience, the best place to do this is at the point of your greatest righteous anger. We have people who are very angry about the fact that there are more than 1,000 orphans in our city. They are in the state's charge because the church has not stepped up to care for them. They are in the state's charge because the demonic forces of child abuse, drug addiction, and domestic violence are running rampant in our city.

Members of our network have chosen to fight and wield their weapons, which are not of this world.[6] When they do, they become the church in a way that causes the devils of hell to tremble. All of a sudden, that promise about the gates of hell not prevailing has new life.

When we find the courage to really begin thinking about the right structures for the church in our time, we realize that whatever we do we have to find a way to mobilize these people to be the church. My fear is that these activists, moved by their righteous anger, will—as they have done for decades—begin to engage this evil without the full support, accountability, and resources of the church. These people are inside every church, but the church is not currently structured to help them with maximum support. So, while they are the church, they are neither received as nor defined in ecclesial terms. This is a devastating mistake.

In time, that disconnect becomes a fatal flaw for the church. Because these leaders, without the full identity and support of the church, either burn out from the work of mission or evolve into something more secular. After all, if the church will not recognize and honor the work they are doing as the work of the church, why should they not look for self-definition and validation elsewhere?

Before you know it, what was meant to be a strong form of church is downgraded to nonprofit charity or community activism, as the sacred things of the church slowly become lost. It is not just that the church is diminished by their noninclusion; these orphaned missionaries are diminished, as well. They forget that they are elders in the church of Jesus Christ. They forget that they are not just fighting for the fatherless to find a home and family, but that they are fighting the ancient battle between good and evil, light and dark, for the kingdom to come, and for the name of Jesus to be made famous. They forget that the only lasting change can come as a subsidiary of the kingdom of God under the Lordship of Jesus Christ. Ironically, this message, while preserved in our prevailing church structures, is not supported by those structures.

The UNDERGROUND is not just a critique of these unengaged forms of church; it is a way of building structures that are able to include, empower, and equip activists to carry the goods of grace into the very real needs of the world. I am not mad at the church; I am mad at the enemy. I love the church, even with its failing structures. I am mad at the devil and his schemes, as they unravel creation and frustrate our intended intimacy with God.

Fighting Principalities

I am reminded of the story of the seven sons of Sceva in Acts 19. They took their chances in a confrontation with the demonic without the tools of the kingdom, and it ended very badly.

> Some Jews who went around driving out evil spirits tried to invoke the name of the Lord Jesus over those who were demon-possessed. They would say, "In the name of the Jesus whom Paul preaches, I command you to come out." Seven sons of Sceva, a Jewish chief priest, were doing this. One day the evil spirit answered them, "Jesus I know, and Paul I know about, but who are you?" Then the man who had the evil spirit jumped on them and overpowered them all. He gave them such a beating that they ran out of the house naked and bleeding.[7]

So it will go for all those who try to take on these grand problems without the authority of the name of Jesus—even more for those who don't really know Jesus, but are somewhat familiar with what he represents. We need the support of the church to help us know and receive the power of his name. It is a fight, but, as Paul explains, "not against flesh and blood, but against the rulers, against the authorities, against the powers of this dark world and against the spiritual forces of evil in the heavenly realms."[8] The real hope is that we would be so close to Jesus and so united in his purpose as a community that we would be like Paul and Peter who were—as strange as it sounds—on a first-name basis with the demons of their neighborhood.

Our whole enterprise is built on a structural foundation of empowerment. That is, we have decided that the very first thing we will do organizationally is serve the sent, and the very first thing the sent need is power, or else they too will end up running away, naked and bleeding.

Empowerment is both internal and external. We need

structures that name, validate, and release people (organizational empowerment) and a spirituality that authorizes and animates us to boldly go into the mission field (spiritual empowerment).

Redefining Leadership

The only way we will get everyone onto the field and into the game to fight is if we change the nature of leadership in the kingdom. Maintaining elitist structures that confine and define leadership as a specialization within the body of Christ limits the potential energy of the church in the pursuit of its mission. The solution is found in Jesus's own definition of leadership. We do not have to find a way to democratize leadership in the kingdom so that everyone can play, because he already has, as Paul describes:

> Have the same mindset as that of Christ Jesus: Who, being in very nature God, did not consider equality with God something to be used to his own advantage; rather, he made himself nothing by taking the very nature of a servant, being made in human likeness. And being found in appearance as a man, he humbled himself by becoming obedient to death—even death on a cross! Therefore God exalted him to the highest place and gave him the name that is above every name, that at the name of Jesus every knee should bow, in heaven and on earth and under the earth, and every tongue acknowledge that Jesus Christ is Lord, to the glory of God the Father.[9]

In this text, Paul calls on us to consider the revelation of Jesus's life as a model for our own, and in that model, we do not just learn about the nature of leadership, we also learn something shocking about God himself. He drops a theological hand grenade here, and it has to do with the forms that Jesus, who is God, takes. On the one hand, he was in being, "very nature God," something the Nicene Creed would render "very God of very God." On the other hand, he became "the very nature of a servant," which begs the question, *Can God take on a nature that is contrary to his own?* If, for instance, God is by nature good, can he take on the nature of evil? Or if God is, in very nature honest, can he take on the nature of dishonesty? Certainly not. Whatever is in the nature of God is immutable and certain.

So what, then, of these two natures of Jesus? If God cannot take on a nature contrary to his own, we are amazed to learn that servanthood is not contrary to his nature. It is a part of it. God is a servant. Compound this bombshell with the word *doulon* in Greek, which is usually rendered "servant." It can just as easily be rendered "slave" here, as it is in other places in the New Testament. To think of God as slave bends the mind, but awakens the soul. It does not diminish God (nothing in his nature can), but it irrevocably elevates servanthood. To serve, then—to make the needs of another more important that one's own—is a part of the nature and beauty of God.

Embracing Servanthood

Movements are born in the soil of self-denial and self-forgetfulness. It's one thing to plant a church, and if you want to one-up a church planter, talk of planting *networks of churches.* Even more ambitious still are church planting movements. But movements, by definition, cannot be led, and they cannot be planned really. They defy control and singular identity. A movement is an egoless enterprise. If a movement happens, it happens because leaders' names are forgotten and no one person or team gets the credit. It must grow out of control. Leaders who aspire to see a movement started, but who are not also ready to abandon their own promotion and fame, are incompatible. One must give way to the other. Simply put, a movement is something God must do, and that means, like John the Baptist understood, "He must become greater, I must become less."[10]

In *The Death of Character*, University of Virginia professor James Davison Hunter observes that the nature of celebrity has changed. There was a time when celebrity status was the reward of achievement. People were well-known because of some distinguishing accomplishment. Today, celebrity status is instead given to performers.[11] People are well-known because they can perform or entertain us. This is true in sports, film, music, and even in the church. We no longer look for our leaders to be men and women whose character is forged through years of faithful service to the people of God. Instead, we are drawn to leaders who can perform well on a stage. The largest churches are led not by the most accomplished leaders, but by the best performers.

This has been missiologically devastating. The church in the West has never been, so it seems, less effective or less potent as salt and light in the world. We are reminded of Jesus's words, "The kingdom of God is not something that can be observed . . . the kingdom of God is in your midst."[12] The kingdom will not—and cannot—come through spectating, because the kingdom is not a spectacle. No matter how large a crowd we gather to watch, it still will not come. Instead Jesus said it comes from exertion, effort, blood, sweat, and tears. It is ushered in by servants, not by celebrities.

Imagine a massive boulder, representing all the evil in the world. No matter how large a crowd we draw to watch the boulder, to mock, to ridicule, or to decry the boulder, it will not move. Some of our churches may have gotten bigger, but the pool of servants exerting force—leaning against the boulder—has gotten smaller. When the church has been led by performers and not by servants, when it has been led by charisma instead of labor, it has failed to mobilize the real power of the church, which is Jesus in his people. Despite all the resources, large churches tend to be less effective (per capita) in evangelism and discipleship,[13] but it does not have to be that way. Even large churches with charismatic communicators can still make themselves small. The way to do this is by servant-leadership.

I know this is true because I am surrounded by an incredible team of servants at the UNDERGROUND. Some of them are especially good at communicating, some are not; some are charismatic, some are not; some are good at raising money, great in a crowd, strategic thinkers, visionaries, and some are not. These gifts, however they present themselves, are secondary realities for us. The first and most significant quality that we look for—and that we reward—is showing up to serve. We are not opposed to people being well-known, but we hope for a caliber of leader who is known for what they have done in service of the body and the kingdom. The authority of Jesus is more like the authority of Mother Teresa, Dorothy Day, William Wilberforce, Dietrich Bonhoeffer, or Martin Luther King, Jr.—people who were not performers, but servants willing to grind, persevere, and even die in the pursuit of their calling. We have people who work in politics, in law, and in city hall, along with people working in jails and under bridges. When we are together, we see very little difference between us, because we are all servants for God's sake.

This is our theological structure. We are led by servants. My staff hears the same question every day: *How can we serve the microchurches?* It is in the water. It is not just a theory for us; it is practical theology, it is a commitment, and it is a way of life. It is the memory of that same refrain, that echo of our leadership commitment: "For what we preach is not ourselves, but Jesus Christ as Lord, and ourselves as your servants for Jesus' sake."[14]

Chapter 10

GOVERNANCE

*Structures, then, are how legitimating
narratives are given material expression in
organizations, groups and societies.*

ALAN J. ROXBURGH

Among other things, the UNDERGROUND is an attempt to find a solution to the conundrum of church governance in our time. To govern is to steward. Each structure and its supporting values, then, must be governed in a way that reinforces the core principles of both. Governance is related to structure in the same way that blood is related to our bodies. It is the faithful and continuous governance of the organism that keeps its parts alive. In our culture, though, we carry a distaste for the idea of church governance because of the cultural imperative not to mix church and government. Further, when we think or talk about politics in the church, it is almost always with disdain. You are more likely to hear someone say that the church "plays" politics and that church government is some kind of corruption of how the church is supposed to be. Yet, it is how we govern that is being critiqued here, not governance itself. Sports fans may rail against the referees for a bad call, but take away the referees (and the rules they enforce), and the sport those fans love vanishes.

The ultimate vision of the Bible is that God himself will one day govern his people, even the whole world.[1] This means God affirms leadership in himself, which implies that it can be holy and good, or at least it can be holy when it is done with a pure heart and with the right people in place. Still, we underestimate the importance of structures for the work of governance—whether for good or ill. For instance, structures that are implicitly biased toward the operation of the church as a Sunday-morning gathering (as the economic model and also the core service provided) will need governance that is geared toward that bias. Making good and godly decisions on how best to lead and steward that structure is the wise and right decision for that system, even if it is still far from the ideal function of the church. Governance does not create structure; it only stewards it. When I sit on a board—whether a nonprofit, church, or business board—the decisions about how to lead are all tied to the purpose of the enterprise. If the goal of the organization is profit, then the board has an ethical obligation to lead toward that goal. That is what they are signing up for.

Western church governance is actually quite good. That is to say, we have done a very good job maintaining a certain structure and approach. For the most part, we maintain, with integrity, the system we have inherited. The people entrusted with those systems have governed them remarkably well, but there are deeper problems. How, for instance, can our current form of middle-class churches effectively reach and include the poor? Many of our churches are economically structured to depend on the offerings their people bring. Poor people, then, are a liability to the model. You can govern that structure as faithfully as possible and never solve that problem. The poor will never really be welcome (not in numbers) because they cannot keep the lights on, pay high salaries, or build a children's wonderland.

I once had a conversation with a young leader who was railing against his church's decision to repave the parking lot. Normally, I would be sympathetic to this kind of frustration, but as I listened,

I found myself seeing the real problem. They were set to spend something like $75,000 on a new surface for a parking lot that was already there—not a huge return on investment, in my opinion. Compounding the problem, this young leader lamented that the church's total annual giving to the poor and external mission work was well below the amount they were spending on pavement. I was sympathetic. I find these kinds of contradictions deeply troubling, but as I asked him more questions about the condition of the parking lot, I began to understand.

All of that church's income comes from offerings collected at the Sunday service. That is their financial model. It is built on a consumer premise. People have a choice in where they worship on Sunday, and in turn, where they give 10 percent (1–2 percent, actually). Therefore, the product they offer is a Sunday-morning experience. If that product suffers—that is, if the parking lot is unusable or in such disrepair that people complain or even stop attending—then there will be no money to spend on anything. Salaries would be in jeopardy. The very existence of the church is dependent on the quality of that Sunday event.

Further, once you own something like a parking lot, you have a responsibility to steward that asset. You have to take care of it. All of a sudden, I could see how that church was possibly making the very best decision, given the system under which it operated. If I were in their shoes, I might actually do the same thing because it's faithful to their structure. (It hurts me to say that.) As much as it would devastate me to spend kingdom money that way, it still might be the right thing to do. Since governance is stewardship of the structures we inherit, good governance is not simply a matter of wisdom, integrity, and biblical faithfulness. It is systemic.

Irish priest and advocate for the poor, Peter McVerry, explains, "Imagine a road with a bad bend. There are many road accidents on that bend, many people are injured. If I am concerned about the suffering of those who are injured there are two possible ways

I can respond."[2] This is the deeper question of all structural and systemic sin. He goes on to say that one can raise money and volunteers for a clinic at the bend, quickly attending to the needs of the accident victims (this is the option that first occurs to us), or one can straighten the road (the option we rarely see). We accept the broken systems we inherit, in many cases, only because we lack the imagination and the will to see them change.

So what do we do when the system in which we operate paints us into such a corner that the best and most responsible thing to do causes us to neglect the poor and deny the greater needs and values of the kingdom? It's a systemic problem. And I am only really exposing the limits of governance in relation to the poor. What about ethnic diversity? Discipleship? Missionary engagement? The just use of money? The system itself must change, or it must go. For instance, the traditional financial model that binds our hands from being generous and expressing the kingdom in our accounting, disbursements, and budgets, is a model that must be rejected if we are to see significant change. Governance then, reinforces the system it maintains. The first step is that we must dismantle and remake the systems of our churches so that our governance bears witness to the fullness of the kingdom. It is this remaking/restructuring that must come first.

Centralized vs. Decentralized Structure

Before we talk about regular church governance, let's focus on this issue of restructuring, which is necessary for many churches in order to be faithful to their sense of mission. The biggest structural decision has to do with the question of centralization. Is the church supposed to be centralized and hierarchical, with clear and streamlined accountability, quality control, and direct-line supervision? Or is the church supposed to be an organic ecosystem that is governed more by processes and by the invisible and sovereign leaders of the Holy Spirit of God? Or is it somehow both? Is it another biblical paradox?

To be sure, there are benefits and biblical precedents for both, and pragmatically, we should be looking for a way to capitalize on both. We should be jealous for the resources of the megachurch. (There is something undeniably powerful about unifying thousands of Christians under one banner—the potential collection of money and marshaling of human resources is staggering.) Further, some ministries are very hard (if not impossible) to pull off without a high level of collaboration and a larger pool of participants. Youth ministry is one example. A house church might only have one teenager in it, while a large church may have dozens. Theological training is hard to imagine in very small grassroots church expressions. These kinds of needs tend to benefit from a centralized structure. Further, there is a multiplier effect in the use of money. The little bit of money I have to give will never, for instance, be enough to buy a facility for hundreds to use or share. But combining my modest giving with the giving of others, we are able to open up new and powerful possibilities.

Still, there are pitfalls with a centralized model like this. Consolidation of resources and programs can also mean consolidation of power. That is almost always a problem for the church leaders who are supposed to serve, give away power, and let Jesus be the head of his church. Further, hierarchy almost always stifles mission in my experience. When a stage is the platform and a few professionals become the *de facto* priesthood, we limit the scope and strength of the church's real engine, which is made up of its people. Big church also means big bureaucracy. Gaining access to those shared resources can be like running the gauntlet, and failure is often the outcome.

On the other hand, small, decentralized church has massive potential for social transformation. It is hard to conceive of the church reaching the whole world without also seeing it freed and released from stifling hierarchies. The idea of church as a decentralized network is not just gaining traction; it seems to be the future. As I said earlier, it is my view that we are speeding toward a future where our most powerful communities will be understood through the lens of network instead of institution. Networks will outnumber hierarchies. The question is not *whether* we will be networked in the coming years, it's *how* we will be networked and *who* will set the terms. As always, when in the midst of a tectonic cultural change, the church has to decide if it will resist the change (and be left on the outside of influencing its expression) or if it will engage the change in order to preach the coming kingdom in the new milieu.

Unfortunately, the church in simple, decentralized form can attract unhealthy leaders and typically lacks the governance required to deal with them. Heresy, demagoguery, spiritual abuse, mismanagement of money, and the like are all threats to small church movements. And of course, there are the always-looming limitations of small communities. When they are at their best, they carry the raw DNA of the kingdom, but when they are not networked together by some real and effective governance, even if they have great potential, they will not last. How then can we capture the empowered entrepreneurial spirit of organic movements while also maintaining healthy oversight and accountability?

Balancing Architecture and Movement

On one end of the spectrum, high church forms are very clear on their governance and invest great authority in the chain of command of their hierarchy. Parish members submit to the judgment of the priest, who submits to the judgment of the bishop, who submits to the archbishop, who submits to the Cardinal, who in turn submits to the Pope, for example. On the other end of the spectrum, house church movements are governed by the principle

of self-regulation, with loose and sometimes nonexistent authority structures and accountability measures. Both extremes have
pitfalls, and even if we cannot think of an actual story of abuse of
power in each case, we can certainly imagine them.

Still, these polarities exist precisely because each approach
has merits and shortcomings. The advantage of a hierarchical
form of governance is clarity and speed. If the hierarchy is godly
and employed in the service of the people, its governance can be
life-giving. Still, power corrupts, and human leaders are notoriously bad at holding this kind of total authority for long periods
of time. Power tends to go to the head and eventually ruins the
leader and their people (of course, there are exceptions). So what
about a more congregational approach?

The advantage here, of course, is the check to any one person's control or exaggerated power. But the cost of decentralized
power is a slow and often impossible gridlock in decision-making.
Governance that gives everyone an equal vote often lacks leadership and vision and binds itself up in the endless battle for elusive
influence. These systems can struggle to do anything new, for
instance, because the bias of the group will always be to maintain
the status quo.

Real reform, then, is very difficult. The democratization of
church governance is built on compromise, and compromise
always means that no one really gets what they want. Because
Jesus is supposed to be the head of his church, it is clear that
whatever we do with regard to governance should somehow
acknowledge him and (as best we understand how) submit to
his leading. Jesus, who sits at the right hand of God, ruling and
reigning,[3] is not simply the idea of a Jewish teacher who we are
to regard as our wise founder. He is still alive, and he is actively
leading his church. Therefore, our governance should be seen as
the discernment and stewardship of that living rule.

Behind the comparisons and polarities lies a deeper question.

What exactly are we trying to govern? Is the church a human hierarchy or a viral movement? Should the prevailing metaphor for the church and its growth be architecture or movement? We have talked about two dominant structures—centralized and decentralized—with all their variations, but what about an alternative to "structure"? What if it's not either-or, but both-and?

Straddling Two Different Structures

At the UNDERGROUND, we have attempted to solve the problem by creating two structures under the same umbrella. We see our work as governing one of two distinct structures with different governing principles. This allows us to put human leadership in its place. Our two-structure approach allows us to centralize those systems that best serve the church from the center, while keeping the practice and identity of the church at large as a decentralized reality. It gives us the advantage of mobilizing strong, lean, nimble apostolic leadership, while simultaneously operating a congregational leadership that gives the Holy Spirit preeminence.

We are not trying to create a hybrid approach through one entity; rather, we are accepting the value of both kinds of structures by embracing them both and organizing ourselves into two complementary, yet distinct, entities. That division of labor then allows us to look at the biblical model of church and the practical realities of mission and allocate our work into one of these two silos: the network of churches on one side and the mission organization on the other.

In turn, we build a firewall between these two structures, so that the one cannot control the other. They operate separate of each other; they are equal in power but not in priority. The church is the real goal, and the agency side exists to serve that living system. The hierarchy that exists in the UNDERGROUND exists in subservience to the organic system. The organization exists

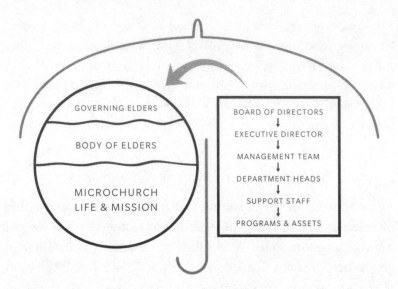

to serve (and not control) the movement. But it must exist. It is both needed and biblical, but only inasmuch as it submits to the advancement of the mission and the kingdom of God, which is the church empowered and released. This is a graphic that represents our model of governance.

The UNDERGROUND community then *is* a collaboration between two structurally complementary entities. On the one hand, the UNDERGROUND exists as an organic network of autonomous microchurches, each united by their agreement to a set of values (the Manifesto) and to a set of standards of character and conduct (eldership and the leadership covenant). On the other hand, the UNDERGROUND is a tightly organized mission agency whose sole purpose is to provide a service platform for microchurches to be planted, equipped, supported, and stimulated to grow and thrive.

I have been critical, even in this book, of Harvard Business School Professor John Kotter's vision-centric prescription for leaders. But to be fair, Kotter wrote his book *Leading Change* in 1988. It is not his fault if people continue to apply principles that are no longer as useful as they once were.

In *Accelerate* (2014), Kotter makes a case for a radical new reorganization of business and nonprofit management structures, what he calls a dual operating system. He sees the challenges and opportunities of the twenty-first century mitigating a whole new way to organize, govern, and lead. His dual operating system thesis is remarkably similar to the basic structure of the UNDERGROUND. Recognizing the changes in our time, he has become critical of what he calls "management driven hierarchies" and sober to their limitations. He is now arguing for networks, not necessarily to replace hierarchies, but to operate as complementary, parallel structures. This dual operating system reflects exactly what we created ten years ago, and it carries many of the same observations and much of the same urgency.

> The world is now changing at a rate at which the basic systems, structures, and cultures built over the past century cannot keep up with the demands being placed on them. . . . The solution is not to trash what we know and start over but instead to reintroduce, in an organic way, a second system—one which would be familiar to most successful entrepreneurs. The new system adds needed agility and speed, while the old one, which keeps running, provides reliability and efficiency. The two together—a dual system—are actually very similar to what all mature organizations had at one point in their life cycles, yet did not sustain (and have long since forgotten).[4]

I can agree with almost every word of this statement when applied to the church. What Kotter calls "the left side" is the traditional structure of the management-driven hierarchy (which in our model is on the right side). What he calls "the right side" is the accelerated network (what we put on the left). The network side is not a subsidiary of the hierarchy, it is made up of free, autonomous, self-directed entrepreneurs. It is more often than not made up of volunteers, and it is where the real life, creativity, and strategic growth of the organization comes from. The hierarchy should exist to serve, provide for, and motivate the network. I was stunned when I first read his book. In some cases, he was using the exact same language we have used for years. If you are intrigued by our structure and governance, I would recommend the whole book to you. Kotter has even become critical of the role of vision in the same way that I have been critical here; what unites the dual system is no longer vision but opportunity. "People who create successful dual systems center the creation of great urgency around opportunity, not vision."[5]

In terms the church can understand, it is the need that drives us, and the meeting of those needs is tied up in the freedom of the network to creatively construct teams with contextualized solutions. But the network still needs the hierarchy. The hierarchy should exist to serve the network, not the other way around. In our parlance, the empowered, decentralized church still needs accountability and support.

Kotter also argues that the natural lifecycle of an organization is to move from network to hierarchy and that the best organizations will create an equilibrium between the two, not remaining a network only, but also not devolving into a hierarchical bureaucracy. This kind of dual system, he maintains, will be necessary for any successful enterprise going forward. It is what our loose church networks need to hear AND what our overmanaged big churches need to hear, as well.

This dual system language mirrors our language of centralized and decentralized, of the organization serving the network, of putting the church on the side of the apostolic. And if we are right, then the single-system hierarchical organization will continue to flounder. In turn, we have to create a dual governance system that creates a healthy exchange between the two systems, getting the best from both and minimizing the weaknesses.

It should be said that I am not proposing a secular system

of governance for the church in our time. On the contrary, I am actually proposing that an experimental expression of the church (the UNDERGROUND)—by reflecting on the original intent of the New Testament and the forces at work in our time and context— have already proposed this selfsame system. The business world is only now (as they have with other concepts like vision, integrity, servanthood, et al.) discovering what we should have known all along. We should not be (nor are we) following them into this new frontier; the church should be leading the way.

The Network of Churches

ELDERS

The basic governance on the organic, networked side of our organ- ization is built on the role of the elder. Since our ecclesiology is so simple (worship, community, and mission), our network empow- ers many initiatives to consider themselves the church. Still, since its inception chronicled in the book of Acts, elders have always led churches. So, we continuously run a year-long class for preparing elders and orienting them to our understanding of the standard for elders laid out in the New Testament and in our own eldership structure and ordination process. Even leaders who do not choose to go through that process are still asked to consider and sign the leadership covenant that holds them to that same standard. Since our eldership model is so flat and empowers so many people, we deal in these documents with the issues of compliance with stated values and standards, the biblical function of discipline (in extreme cases), and maintaining a standard of historic orthodoxy. Because of these issues, there must exist a smaller body to govern the whole.

With so many microchurches in the network, there is the potential to have hundreds of elders. This body of Elders then becomes accountable to each other. This happens primarily through our leadership covenant. We covenant with each other to maintain the Manifesto, to cultivate our relationship with God, and to never exploit our people or do anything that could harm the reputation of Jesus and his people. And if we ever do, we agree to humbly submit to loving confrontation and even discipline. The covenant is made of self-evident things. There is really nothing controversial in it; we just ask leaders to commit to all the things to which good leaders already want to commit. This simple act of covenant has proven to be remarkably powerful for us in helping to keep people honest, committed, and perseverant.

Still, there will always be problems. People sin, and the devil is real. So, when there is an accusation leveled against one of the microchurch leaders, there must be a smaller group of people who serve to adjudicate the issue.

GOVERNING ELDERS

This smaller group of elders represents the most respected members from the larger body of elders. They are the elders of elders. Their role is to monitor and maintain the values and standards agreed to by the whole body. They also represent the final line of authority over the elders themselves in theological concerns, conduct, and character matters, as well as anything pertaining to the role and position of an elder. They would, therefore, carry no authority in the day-to-day ministry practice, strategy, or autonomy of the microchurches and their leadership. The governing elders retain the roles of approving the ordination of all new elders, disciplining elders in cases of misconduct or moral failing, and in extreme and dire cases, removing elders.

We think about these governing elders as overseers. This term is almost interchangeable with the word elder in Paul's use, which is partly why these people are chosen from the body of elders. We do not see them as something other than, or above the other elders, but rather as people who carry the respect of their peers, with the reputation, wisdom, and temperance needed to listen to accusations and adjudicate fairly.

THE MISSION ORGANIZATION

BOARD OF DIRECTORS AND THE EXECUTIVE DIRECTOR

So the UNDERGROUND is an organic decentralized network, but it is also a mission agency and a fully functioning nonprofit organization. In that sense, it operates from a clear and plain organizational chart. The executive director is hired by and accountable to the board of directors. This board works to empower and support the director in the pursuit of the organizational mission. The purpose of this side of the UNDERGROUND is to inspire, serve, and support the other side. The 501(c)3 exists solely to see people in ministry free and empowered to realize the missional dreams God has given them.

The organizational (centralized) side then exists to serve the growth and development of the microchurches. This is the board's purpose, to which they hold our executive director and all the staff accountable. Their organizational success is rooted solely in the success of the ministries in the organic family of autonomous microchurches. So, the organizational hierarchy exists entirely to serve so the grassroots work of the microchurches doesn't need to focus on administration at a high level. This is the side of the dual system that relates to the government, that complies with all the necessary regulations, and where all liability and assets are stored. In order for the network to be truly free, both from logistical burdens and from liability concerns, the organization has to operate with impeccable integrity and foresight. This side thinks through everything from policy and protocols, to liability and worst-case scenario planning. These concerns, which are usually constraining to the free-flowing life of an organic system, are then quarantined (mostly) into this side of the enterprise.

Each of these governing bodies is fully empowered to serve in distinct and complementary ways. While the governing elders are tasked with the biblical expectations and spiritual leadership of the elders and ordination (character, conduct, and doctrine), the board of directors and, in turn, the executive director and staff are tasked with legally operating the organization itself.

THE PLACE OF CHURCH DISCIPLINE

So far, our discussion of governance has focused on high-level structures and systems. But what about where the rubber meets the road? What does governance actually look like on a day-to-day level? The body of Christ offers an important analogy for understanding the church, because we all have a physical body. Let me use this analogy to talk about the practices of church governance.

In 2015, I took a three-month Sabbatical from ministry in Tampa, Florida, to stay in Charlottesville, Virginia. One of my sabbatical goals was to give some serious attention to my physical body. I like sports, and for most of my life, I have exercised here and there, but I had never really appreciated the gift a healthy and strong body can be until this sabbatical. I have only one body, after all, and I thought maybe I should try to see if I could get it to its best possible condition. It is interesting that trying to focus on taking better care of my body necessarily meant pushing it to its brink, even "hurting" it—muscles must be "broken down" in order to get stronger. Of course, I ate better and tried to get more sleep too, since I was generally more aware of what affects my corporeal home. But the real work of taking care of a body is exercise.

I got to the point where I was doing two workouts each day: a five-mile run in the morning (with all of those accursed Virginia hills) and 60–90 minutes of hard-core cardio circuit training. At first, it was—how should I put it—nauseating, but near the end,

I felt a lot stronger and certainly more capable. The work itself never stopped being painful, though. To notice that this kind of pain is both self-inflicted and does some kind of long-term good was to stumble on a deeper truth.

Most of us neglect exercise (even when we are trying to do it) because we prefer instant gratification. We don't like a little pain for a lot of gain if that gain comes at some later time. If we have ever committed to exercise, we at least know what we are giving up when we fail to workout. So when we don't exercise, we know we aren't being healthy, and so we make our endless procrastinating promises that tomorrow, next week, or one day we will get around to it. This whole process made me reflect on the other body I live in.

The body of Jesus Christ is the weightiest and, at times, deformed body we live in.

As I think about the stewardship of Jesus over his own body, I can see that pain and trial is not as often the work of the enemy as we might suppose. In fact, it is his loving way. If he were to shelter us from any kind of suffering, he would make his body somehow weaker and less stable in the world. The words of God and the gospel of his kingdom are broad and weighty burdens, and the shoulders of his body need to be broad enough and strong enough to bare them. More than that, I think we are supposed to be this world's chief example of virtue. Things like compassion and endurance are our birthright, but what are those virtues if not impossibly heavy burdens? We simply cannot be his body in the world without the muscles and lungs to bare these great weights and to carry them over long distances. When the New Testament writer James says, "Consider it pure joy, my brothers and sisters, whenever you face trials of many kinds,"[6] he may have been thinking about the invaluable outcome of broader, stronger shoulders to carry the burdens of the church, "because you know that the testing of your faith produces perseverance."[7]

Pain that comes from evil men or a broken world then is not something to run from; rather, it is something that prepares us for the work of carrying a cross. A burden though it is, a cross is lighter still than a life without it.

The word "discipline" has two massively different connotations in the church. On the one hand, we are taught that "spiritual disciplines" are the bedrock of intimacy and connection to God. Daily and regular spiritual practices like prayer, fasting, giving, service, and worship make up the very best experiences that the church has to offer. On the other hand, "church discipline" is something very dark and foreboding. It is not something you ever hope to experience, and when it happens to you, one can only assume it is because of some deeply deviant behavior. There are those who lament the decline of church discipline as a sign that we have lost our backbone or biblical courage, while others lament church discipline as yet another example of the way we have damaged people with an inappropriate use of control and power.

What persons on either side of that debate may be missing, though, is the deeper truth that the two uses are not so different. Spiritual disciplines (when really practiced) are difficult. In many ways, they break us. And church discipline (when practiced well) is quite freeing and beautiful. Spiritual disciplines require more breaking down than we admit, but it is ultimately for the rebuilding and restoration of something that we lost or do not have in our current state of existence. Likewise, in cases of church discipline, the breaking has already happened, and mostly that process is set on restoration too. Both are about breaking and restoring, about humbling and exalting, about repentance and renewal.

To govern the church (as with governing our individual selves) is to discipline it. The body that is disciplined is a strong body. It is capable, versatile, and brave. It has stamina, as well as strength. The church that is undisciplined—or ungoverned—is frail, self-centered, and ultimately of very little use in the world.

I think about the Yerkes-Dodson law, named after the early twentieth-century psychologists that determined we perform better with more challenge, but only up to a point. They noticed that performance increases as tension is applied (what they called arousal), but at some point (what they called optimum performance), adding more tension begins to decrease performance. In other words, the harder something is, the more we rise to the challenge of it and the better we do. This holds true until it is too hard, and then performance declines. Too much, and we break; too little, and we are bored. They concluded that we tend to perform best at an optimum point of strain.

This helps illuminate the two connotations of discipline. It frees, and it challenges. When you exercise, the key is to know your limits and to push yourself just to the edge of them but never

YERKES DODSON LAW

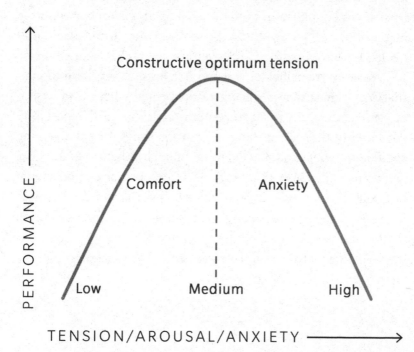

farther than that. Ruin waits for people who push themselves beyond what their bodies can bear.

This also is a promise Jesus makes: the burden he places on his body will never exceed his grace and, therefore, our capacity to carry it. So, too, is the responsibility of those who would govern it. We hold the important tension of freedom and responsibility. In the UNDERGROUND, we honor both of those virtues by our two-structured paradox, and as long as they are both honored, we have seen that somehow the expressions of church among us thrive. Governance, then, is the attempt to create equilibrium—to set in place discipline and practices that do not inhibit us from the freedom of movement and of ministry, while also holding us to its standards and expectations.

It is not my intention to push or promote our style of governance upon any particular church. On the contrary, I would hope that even better examples than ours might emerge to hold these tensions in equilibrium. I only offer it as an example of how we might have the courage to ask these questions of the governance models we have inherited and, even more, move to change them.

We are responsible for this too. We have to set about to marshal governance that is freeing to the people whom God has, in point of fact, already freed and empowered. Our goal, in part, is to not stand in the way of that, while at the same time challenging and holding the people of God to the standard that his grace, love, and holiness demand. God is good, and the people of God should be a collective representation of that good in the world. Jesus does not need us to rule; he is doing that, but he does need us to listen to him and to announce his rule in the world around us. This is the work of governance and stewardship in the kingdom.

Chapter 11

SACRAMENTS

But he said to me, "My grace is sufficient for you."

THE APOSTLE PAUL[1]

Liturgy in a loose sense is the habits of our regular life that form who we are. What we do each day and each week is the very liturgy of our life. We structure our lives with practices to reinforce the things we hold most dear. If our practices are less than ultimately meaningful—sports, entertainment, or television—we may need to do some soul searching. It is also possible that the things that fill our lives—work, family, calling, community, and the like—are reflections of a deep structure that pleases God.

Communities have liturgies too—that is, the formal or informal agreement of how to live in the pursuit of God and his grace. We all structure our lives in pursuit of what we consider sacred. The deep structure of churches includes this understanding of the sacramental life of followers of Jesus. Since the UNDERGROUND is a community defined by its common pursuit of mission, it is an interesting exercise to notice what we have come to find sacred. Unlike other principles and practices that we set out to embody, these missional sacraments are more of a recent revelation for me.

The longer we walk together on the road less traveled, the more we also discover the parts of Christian practice that are timeless and transcendent. As we do, we can see that in certain practices the grace of God seems to be always present. The church has traditionally considered that phenomenon sacramental. Sacraments are "efficacious signs of grace, instituted by Christ and entrusted to the church, by which divine life is dispensed to us."[2] That is, sacraments are practices Jesus affirmed that are not only fruitful and valuable, but when we do them together, they always deliver grace and joy. The practitioner does not necessarily even need to have faith or correct motivation—although such things certainly matter—for the act to carry grace and transfer something good into the life of the one who experiences it.

So it stands to reason that if we want more grace in this world and in our lives, we should practice sacraments more often. We should make them an essential part of all of our ministries, our homes, our teams, and even our strategies. I want to unpack some of the most common practices here as a kind of informal structure for the missionary church.

The Roman Catholic Church codified its list of seven sacraments in the sixteenth century at the Council of Trent:

- The sacraments of initiation: baptism, confirmation, and Eucharist,
- The sacraments of healing: confession and anointing the sick, and
- The sacraments of service: ordination and marriage.

However, the contention was that they were only naming what Jesus had already instituted and practices that seem to have always carried grace in them.

Protestants typically only argue for two sacraments: baptism and communion. Whatever sacraments make your list, the process of trying to ask and answer the question of what is a sacrament is a powerful one. I contend that every generation of the church should consider and conspire to answer the question of sacraments. That consideration too, as with so many questions, should involve the intersection between traditional orthodox Christian experience and contextual realities. I have given the matter serious and sustained thought, yet, I confess, the matter is far from settled for me. Still, I think I can discern five missional sacraments that have always been present for us—five things Jesus has given us to do, in which we always experience grace.

Ordination: Cultivating a Covenantal Leadership Community

When we returned from the Philippines in the fall of 2007, we were composed of seventeen microchurches. Of course, those groups were not conceived overnight. They represented years of work that many of our core people were doing up until the formation of the UNDERGROUND. Even so, about half of those were new groups, birthed out of the missionary core that has existed since our inception. We rented a small office in the inner-city neighborhood where many of us lived. It was about 1,500 square feet, and we built it out to serve as an office/co-op for five of those ministries and as a gathering place for everyone to use. We had two staff members—a part-time person to help with financial services and me. One of the first things we did was to convene an elders-in-training course that would meet once a month for a year. And this choice, even then, seemed odd and out of place for us.

Once you accept our simple ecclesiology, you will uncover churches where you least expect them. Lots of things we weren't calling church actually were, and from our reading of the New Testament, we were convinced that each church was supposed to be led by elders (not pastors, which is a gifting). Ephesians 4 outlines the office or role of the pastor/shepherd as one of five kinds of leaders that have been given to the church and charged with her equipping and edification. To have chosen only one of those as the singular title for church leadership would not only be in error, it would also be dangerously restrictive. Instead of one gift being elevated and equated with ecclesial leadership, the early church seemed more interested in a character standard for its leaders. In other words, it wasn't what gift you had that mattered, it was your maturity and character that determined if you were a suitable leader for the people of God. This was a revolutionary idea for us.

Paul goes out of his way in two of his epistles to leave us with a particular character description and standard for future generations to uphold.[3] We were convinced that the church was supposed to be led by elders. The root word he uses implies simply the older ones. It is so elegant and so important to identify people who have simply walked a little farther down the road than the rest of the community. Because we were so young, we had to interpret this title as a relative trait. That is to say, when a microchurch gets started, someone is the eldest, the most mature. That person then needs to understand the significance of their role in that community. Our simple definition of church meant that we were going to need a whole lot of elders. Every microchurch needed at least one, maybe more. And we needed to do the work of order— ordination—to make sure that those older ones knew their place, authority, and responsibility.

So, strangely, one of the first things we did as an expression of alternative church was to ordain twenty-seven elders. We crafted a class that would not so much make people elders as orient elders to the biblical expectation of the office they were already holding. God calls people to be elders, and they confirm that calling in how they live and lead. In my view, the role of apostle in the New Testament was to lay on their hands as an act of confirmation. Someone older sees the traits and calling of an elder in them and ordains that. Even a twenty-five-year-old that runs a church for at-risk kids can see himself as an elder. With that moniker comes both authority and responsibility. It is an honor and a burden, but one we were all ready and willing to bear. No one was running away from responsibility. If anything, we understood that standing on our own, like we were, exposed us to risk and failure from things we just could not even conceive. You don't know what you don't know.

So, we knew we needed to prepare our young contingent of released autonomous leaders for the gravity of what they were doing. Once you validate these small expressions of the church, you have to quickly establish the terms of their autonomy. It is a paradox that we need to both free these leaders and also impress upon them the responsibility that their freedom implies. If you want to free people to do what God has called them to do, how then do you impress on them the importance of submission to authority and an understanding that in certain matters they must stand alone as answerable to God?[4]

Good leaders desire both freedom and accountability, because good leaders know they need both. As servants of these leaders, it is our responsibility to provide them with both. No one is advocating anarchy; on the contrary, I would say that the accountability framework in our network is possibly more robust than with traditional church. We crave grace-filled accountability, without the control. The problem too many of us had experienced before is that when the churches we were part of wanted to practice accountability—whether doctrinal or practical—it ended up looking like control and dominance. It is an approach that, in our minds, is totally inappropriate for human leadership in the kingdom of God. So, we began to create a community that operated in what Dee Hock famously called a "chaord."

As the enigmatic founder of the company Visa, Hock was one of the pioneers of the creator economy. The ubiquitous Visa brand offered a new kind of business that didn't *produce* anything. Visa simply offered an innovation to banks that was theirs to use as they saw fit, as long as that use fell within certain governing guidelines. Hock would go on to reflect on his groundbreaking business model, describing it as "order" in "chaos"—a chaord. Freedom is given to banks to develop credit programs with terms and rates that are up to them, while adhering to the definitional standard of what it means to be Visa. He imagined a series of values running like a spine through the chaos of an environment, giving it the strength of both the liberated and the regulated system. He was able to create a company with billions in revenue while doing virtually nothing. In an entrepreneurial world enamored with iconoclasts, Dee Hock stands apart as a shy alternative who actually out-innovated most of the icons we can name.

Hock described a chaord as "any self-organizing, self-governing, adaptive, nonlinear, complex organism, organization, community or system, whether physical, biological or social, the behavior of which harmoniously blends characteristics of both chaos and order."[5]

We didn't know it when we began, but we were creating a chaordic system—a version of the church that operated under the same conditions as Hock's chaord. We were attempting to capitalize on the creativity and passion of every person (freedom), while also building a discernible community that was growing and accountable to itself and a greater goal (responsibility).

One of the outcomes of that first class of elders was the desire and need to covenant together toward a certain standard of character and conduct. These terms (along with our radical values) became the glue that held us together. We understood ourselves to be free, autonomous leaders, empowered by Jesus himself to reach and love parts of our city, yet we knew we were more than that. We were (and are) members of a body, and as such we were responsible to each other. We knew that and needed to say so somehow.

While we were governed by a spirit of adventure in those days and a "fly by the seat of your pants" ethic, this commitment to something bigger, to each other, needed something concrete to seal it. We decided to actually ordain our elders. We knew this would be the first of many classes. Hundreds of leaders would come to understand themselves not just as microchurch planters, but as elders in the church itself.

We knew that the gravity of ordination needed a corresponding gesture. We also knew our ordination could not be something that was hierarchical, which would have been a contradiction. And besides, who would fain to hold that kind of authority? From where would it be derived? It had to come from a condition that already existed. God makes people elders; we don't. We simply note and confirm it. It had to be collegial, confirmed not by some hierarchy, but by the body of elders already faithfully at work in the community. It had to be based on demonstrated character, not charisma or gifts.[6]

We have not asked all of our leaders to go through that ordination process, but we wish they would. We simply do not require it (because we generally don't require things). Still, we know that what they are really doing as leaders of the church is performing the office of an elder. We do ask all of our leaders to agree to our covenant, which also includes all the aspiration of the Manifesto and more.[7]

When I talk about ordination, a part of the sacramental life of the missionary community, I am not really talking about ceremony. Ordination is not a ceremony, although it often is so important in the life of a believer that it warrants one. All people lack authority on their own. True authority, by its nature, cannot be self-derived; it must be bestowed. In turn, all people are looking for that transaction. We are looking for someone who holds authority to trust us with it. We crave that as deeply as we crave belonging and love. I am sure this is why Jesus's final gift to his followers was the gift of his authority. To be sent as an emissary of one who is greater to go and do in their name is something that is necessary for human wholeness and fulfillment.

The paradox of leadership in the kingdom is to simultaneously carry the authority of the kingdom and experience what C. S. Lewis calls "the specific pleasure of the inferior," "of a child before his father, a creature before its creator."[7] That yearning, that search and hope for a word of praise or affirmation is actually a godly yearning. It is a child's desire to hear their Father say, "Well done." Even Jesus was ordained into ministry by this word of blessing, love, and empowerment from heaven.

So we ordain ordinary people. We call them leaders and give them authority to lead in his name. We do this because they are capable and already are elders, because this is the only way we will win the whole world, because Jesus has already empowered them and we are agreeing with him, and because it is a part of healing, loving, and saving them.

Communion Table: Participating in the Presence of Christ Jesus Through the Gospel Received

I find that the degree to which our missionary people are healed from the wounds inflicted from previous church experiences is the degree to which they are open to rediscovering the grace of certain historical church practices. Still, these discoveries are less about returning to a particular tradition and more about contextualizing grace, in all its forms. For instance, the discipline of the Lord's Supper is something that we have practiced weekly as a community since our inception. We embrace the practice in all its forms.

David Fitch, in his beautiful book *Faithful Presence*, outlines three spaces in which we embrace the Eucharist, spaces he calls "circles."[8] The closed circle is the formal expression of the table, which most churches experience in some way, and around which certain high church forms build their liturgy. The second circle is open. It is the table of our homes, where those who believe and those who do not yet believe can all break bread and discern the presence of Jesus. Finally, the third space, which he calls the half circle, is the place of mission. In this space, we are guests, but we still bring the Eucharist with us and, in turn, the presence of Jesus. I so appreciate Fitch because he gives language to both the depth and breadth of communion as we have experienced it. In the UNDERGROUND, we have always practiced the rehearsal and remembering of the broken body and shed blood of Jesus in all three of these spaces. We come to the table every week when we gather; we come to the table in our homes; and we bring the grace of the table to the streets and into places of mission.

Living in intentional Christian community, as we do, and living in the inner city, surrounded by people in need, it is no exaggeration to say that I have shared the grace of my dinner table thousands of times. It would be impossible for me to quantify the ministry that has happened around the chicken, rice, and beans lovingly prepared by my wife, Monica. We have laughed, worshiped, cried, argued, evangelized, repented, and basically lived out the whole of the kingdom at that table. Still, it never grows old. When Jesus is remembered, at any table, he is present and there is grace.

This last year, we prepared a simple meal for our microchurch on the Wednesday before Thanksgiving. There were maybe twelve people sitting around the table that night, three being new guests. I think that two of them were not followers of Jesus. Still, we went around the table and gave thanks for something. When it came to the two nonbelievers, through tears, each in their own way they said, "What I am most thankful for is this, being here with all of you." We have seriously miscalculated the potency of biblical hospitality in the witness of the church. We have, but Jesus has not.

Of all the ritual acts that Jesus could have instituted, this alone was his command to us: to remember him over the breaking of the bread. Every time we gather as a missionary community (in a larger worship setting), we serve communion. The tables of our homes are not a derivation of the thing we have always done at church; rather, the small token of a meal that we serve in our churches is an attempt to capture what happens in our homes. Both are powerful in their own way. But the bread broken in mission and in evangelism and around our family tables is the same as the bread we break in worship. At least it can be.

It is worth considering why Jesus, who was somewhat averse to the formation of a new law, would insist on this one ritual practice. It must have something to do with the self-perpetuating importance of memory. The kingdom cannot advance without remembering it, without remembering Jesus. It is the cross he wants them to remember. In the great commission, he gives his disciples the task of teaching people all that he had commanded, so clearly he wanted them to remember it all—but the cross was to be remembered every time they gathered. In other words, Jesus is saying I know you cannot recount and rehearse everything about me every time you see each other, but if you remember just one thing, remember that I was broken and given to you. I am your sustenance. I am your Passover. I am your atonement. It is a gory image that we are meant to hold in our minds forever.

Yet, inside that one command, inside this one gesture is everything that is important for Christian community. He suffered because we are sinners, because of our hatred toward God and goodness itself. Never forget that. He suffered because he loves—he loves us with the fire of a thousand suns. Never forget that. He suffered to purchase our lives, to ransom us from sin and the devil. We are therefore totally free, but we are also totally his. Never forget that. He suffered for the whole world, even your enemies and the people who don't agree with you. We are unified by this great sacrifice, unified in our neediness and our salvation. Never forget that.

It is no coincidence that the Last Supper takes place on Passover. They are celebrating the Seder, which begins with the heart-stopping question of memory, gratitude, and worship, "How is this night different from all other nights?" It is different because we were once slaves, and on this night, he made us free. That question echoes in our hearts every time we break bread together, every time we remember the night he was betrayed. So even though we may do it a thousand-thousand times, it never grows old.

Repentance and Reconciliation: Living with Humility as We Bring People to God

I pair reconciliation with repentance as one sacrament. While at first I wanted to consider just reconciliation as the next missional sacrament—the process of lamenting, forgiving, and restoring relationships that have been broken—I see now that reconciliation is not possible without repentance, which itself is sacramental. Like the body and the blood, so too are repentance and reconciliation part of the same sacrament. It is repentance for the purpose of reconciliation. Saying sorry is fulfilled when you are restored to relationship, any relationship, with God or with people.

Elsewhere, writing about my two-decade-long experience of living in intentional community, I made this argument:

> We thrive in community. In collaboration we are at our best as a people. Conversely, our greatest evils as a people are produced by isolation and fragmentation of human community. The kiss of God upon our souls was community, and the curse of sin and our partnership with evil is fragmentation. The great work of the enemy in the world is the work of fracturing, dividing, breaking. The enemy cannot, like God, and like you and I (who are made in the image of God) create. The enemy can only corrupt that which is created. He can only fragment it, breaking it into less and less glorious God-revealing pieces. This is, grossly stated, what the Devil does in the world.

God, on the other hand, who first gave us community with each other and with him, is at work also in the world. And his work is to heal, reconcile, and restore that which is broken, fragmented, and fractured into what it was intended to be. Simply put, God makes things whole again. The recent theological interest in the Hebrew notion of shalom (often translated "peace") has become a helpful rubric for the intention of God in the world. The term is richer and deeper than that one English connotation, as it actually sounds the depths of the human longing not just for the end of hostility (peace), but for the restoration of all things to their intended state, wholeness, and harmony with God and others. The hope of human beings and the mission of God, it could be said, is to bring peace to the hostility of the enemy and wholeness to all that is broken. The New Testament equivalent of shalom is what Jesus called the kingdom of God. It is not just a spiritual reign, or a political reign, it is so sweeping and comprehensive, that the term is meant to include all things. It is, again, the healing of every world system and every broken thing in the universe. It is that significant.

The dream of the kingdom of God is a dream of community. And the good news of the kingdom of God is what Paul called "the message of reconciliation." Jesus came to accomplish the dual purpose of reconciliation (reconciling the world to God, and people to each other) and to destroy all the works of the evil one. Because reconciliation means the end of division.[9]

Our community has found that through our subservience to the mission of God, we have no choice but to start with the humility of the limitations of our own work. All of our relationships are marred by the weakness of our flesh and the faintness of our hearts. Reconciliation is the goal of all our work, and reconciliation is impossible without repentance, so we baptize our lives in it.

We are like Peter who resists the cleansing touch of Jesus at first but, once he understands that there is no way to be a part of the kingdom of God without it, wants his whole body washed.[10] No one wants to admit they are wrong—that the way they are currently doing ministry or relating to people is wrong—but without the courage to face both of those realities, the power of the kingdom remains beyond our reach.

What we have come to see is that the feedback loop of humility, repentance, and reconciliation not only brings the kingdom into those difficult moments, but it sanctifies us in the process. This is how human beings grow. Repentance is not something you do once. It is something that should drench our lives, especially if we imagine ourselves as witnesses to the kingdom. We will not, in the end, captivate the world by our righteousness, but by longing for his. Repentance opens the door to the room of reconciliation, first in our own brokenness with God, but ultimately in the devastation that is human brokenness.

I believe in the kingdom more each day. I see the beauty, wisdom, and greatness of Jesus a little more each day because I have learned to repent—and because I experience life in a community of people who know how to say they were wrong. Humility is spiritual intelligence. It is the openness to the paradox of our status as both saint and sinner. We know we are broken, sinful, and hopeless without him, and yet, we also know we are chosen, loved, and destined. The former keeps us from pride, and the later from despair.

This sacrament, more than any other, has built my personal faith, and its continued embrace is the key to keeping our teams and marriages together, to surviving in ministry, and finally, to growing as a person.

Incarnation: Embracing the Incarnation as Missionaries

A great deal has been written about the role of incarnation in the work of mission. It is impossible to imagine Christology without the incarnation. It is the model of mission for who would come after him. In a general sense, the incarnation of Jesus is the humiliation of God. He cannot die if he does not condescend to take on flesh. He becomes one of us to save us. He is God become poor to save us from our poverty.

In the later part of the first century, when there were still living people who had known and walked with Jesus in the flesh, they were still trying to make sense of it all. Who had they actually encountered? John, one of the last disciples to die, marveled, "We have seen with our own eyes . . . our hands have touched . . . the Word of life."[11] John 1, then, is his attempt to reach the fullness of this visitation, mirroring Genesis 1 and the very creation of the world: "In the beginning was the Word, and the Word was with God, and the Word was God. He was with God in the beginning. Through him all things were made; without him nothing was made that has been made."[12]

"Not only does God speak to humankind," the Scottish theologian John Knox reflects, "but the divine speech has become a human person."[13]

God saves us through the mission of incarnation. He takes on the flesh and lives in the community of the people he proposed to love, ransom, and save. In the same way, incarnation can be applied to the missionary. Jesus says in John 20, "As the Father has sent me, I am sending you."[14] Our apostleship is not just tied to the authority of Jesus, but also the model of Jesus. To do mission without incarnation will always fail to communicate a faithful witness to the truth of the God revealed in Jesus.

I have lived in the same inner-city neighborhood since 1996, but I have never considered myself an urban missionary. I have probably had 100 ministry conversations with the urban poor in my neighborhood over the years. I have broken up fights, intervened in domestic violence, cared for a woman recovering from having been raped, and shared the gospel with people who were high, enraged, or just plain crazy. I have given shelter, help, and comfort to countless people over the years—just because of where we live. We have shared the gospel, led people to Jesus, cast out demons, healed the sick, and seen miracles. And yet, I have never set out—not one day of my life—to do urban ministry. All of that happened simply because of the decision to move into the neighborhood. That one choice to move my body into a place among the needy, and my first commitment to be a herald of the kingdom, was all it took. We are just trying to be good neighbors in a neighborhood that needs good neighbors.

This is the radical simplicity of the incarnation as a missiological principle and the grace of the incarnation as a missiological sacrament. Whenever we enter into the world, into the lives of the people we are called to reach, grace is waiting for us. Our willingness to sit at the bar, get in the ditch, move into the neighborhood, walk onto the campus, step on the court—all these trigger some sort of movement from God. To be a missionary is to be sent, and going always invites God more deeply into our lives. Even when we stumble through it, even when we cannot find the words, our presence is already communicating something critical about God and about our intentions.

In Matthew 25, Jesus says that whatever you do to the least of these, you have done for me.[15] He intertwines his intimate presence with the poor, the captive, and the lost as the objects of our mission. In short, if and when we go to them and love them where they are, he promises us an encounter with him. It is nothing short of breathtaking. The modern church seems to continue thinking that Jesus is most profoundly encountered through music and surrounded by other Christians. As beautiful as that is, it is nothing compared to the promise of his presence in the sacrament of incarnation.

Proclamation: Preaching the Presence of the Kingdom

I have been trying to articulate the gospel to lost people since I was a teenager. From my early years doing open air evangelism on the campus at the University of Florida to sharing through more sophisticated apologetic forums, I have never lost my zeal to see Jesus known, loved, and obeyed. In spite of my own failures as a preacher and the many rejections I have suffered, I can honestly say that I have never felt anything other than the pleasure of God when I was doing this work.

Every time we preach the good news to someone who has not heard or who has not accepted it by faith, God is present with us. Even if we do not do it perfectly, I still think he is pleased. To this day, I feel the butterflies in my stomach, as if the kingdom hangs in the air and eternity in the balance, because I know that it actually does. In that rare and beautiful moment when someone turns, God descends in a way like no other, and the kingdom has come. It has come to them and to the preacher because they shared. It is the closest thing to a drug in ministry. It hits like a high. Even when I have made a mess of it, I feel that closeness, that grace from the God who sent me. I cannot think of anything that we can do in this life that is more important or more filled with real and potential joy than evangelism.

Even though many Christians would agree and confirm this experience with their own stories of bumbling obedience, we still neglect this grace. Please understand, whatever we can say about the gospel—that it must be lived, that it must be supported by love, that it must be clearly presented, that it must be orthodox— whatever our view on evangelism, the gospel is preached. It is also lived, embodied, and experienced in the heart, but all these are subject to the first truth—it is experienced only if it is first preached.

You are not living the gospel, not experiencing the fullness of God, and certainly not being a missionary if you are not preaching the gospel. Preaching is how the world will know. You cannot believe if you have never heard, and you cannot hear if someone is not willing to preach. We neglect this simple logic, and I'm convinced that we do it out of our own fear.

I do not say this to condemn. On the contrary, preaching, too, is a sacrament of the missionary community. It promises grace to you if you will only practice it as a part of the rhythms of your life. When we as a church, nonprofit, or community neglect it, we are denying ourselves grace. There are remarkable activist communities and Christians who collaborate for kingdom purposes, but for whatever reason, whether intentional or incidental, they do not practice the sacrament of proclamation. Aside from being disobedient, it resigns that community to death after one generation. One of my missionary mentors in the Philippines asked me, "Brian, how will you build a church that lasts 1,000 years?" That is the question. Without proclamation, there will be no church after one generation, never mind 1,000 years.

Paul says it perfectly in Romans 10:8–15:

> "The word is near you; it is in your mouth and in your heart," that is, the message concerning faith that we proclaim: If you declare with your mouth, "Jesus is Lord," and believe in your heart that God raised him from the dead, you will be saved. For it is with your heart that you believe and are justified, and it is with your mouth that you profess your faith and are saved. As Scripture says, "Anyone who believes in him will never be put to shame." For there is no difference between Jew and Gentile—the same Lord is Lord of all and richly blesses all who call on him, for, "Everyone who calls on the name of the Lord

will be saved." How, then, can they call on the one they have not believed in? And how can they believe in the one of whom they have not heard? And how can they hear without someone preaching to them? And how can anyone preach unless they are sent? As it is written: "How beautiful are the feet of those who bring good news!"

Chapter 12

MONEY

Frugality includes all the other virtues.

CICERO

W hat is it with money? Friendships, marriages, ministries, careers all fall before money. Jesus talked a lot about it. He seemed to understand what we don't—that money and its use are somehow connected to our hearts and, therefore, to our relationship with God. Money is not evil, per se, but the pursuit of wealth is a dead-end for the human heart. In the pursuit of wealth, we discover not only its inadequacy for making us happy or whole, but we discover just how dark our hearts really are. Greed and financial ambition expose our depravity and deception in a way that few things can. How then can we talk about a Christocentric life, a missional church, or a radical expression of the kingdom without considering the use of money?

Often tied to our church structures, the way we gather and disperse money reveals something about who we are and what we care about. More than that, it can trap us in systems we don't want to stay in because our model depends on our financial status. So, even if leaders and their people are ready for real and radical change, that is only likely if the financial model is addressed.

When it comes to money, many of our decisions are already made by the systems we inhabit, as with the story of the church parking lot project I mentioned above. Still, at some point, even though our systems can force our hand, we have to be responsible for how we steward money. In addition to the resurfacing story, I have also heard about a church in Canada that chose to tear up their parking lot in order to turn the area into a community garden. Every safe can be cracked, every prison escaped. Systemic limitations aside, we also have to ask ourselves if we have the will to spend money differently. If you are coming from a traditional church model and want to cultivate the kind of community I am describing, there should be no delusions—you will have to completely rethink how you use and relate to money.

I am talking about the leader who wants to do better, who wants to be more generous, and who sees the great economic disparity between God's people around the world, but also feels trapped by the inherited financial model. What do they do next?

Those leaders have to reimagine a church that is not dependent on certain ministry models that require money to be spent in certain ways. We have to move away from those old wineskins because they are no longer effective, but we also have to move away from them because they have caused us to be something less than holy in our use of money.

More Than Tithing

There is a real irony (if not hypocrisy) in hearing churches and church leaders pontificate on the importance of personal tithing, only to discover that that same church does not practice what it preaches. Asking American Christians, in particular, to give 10 percent of their income is a good idea. If 90 percent of us would give 10 percent of our income, we could raise more than $85 billion each year on top of what is currently given.[1] This could solve massive global problems. But even if we could accomplish that kind of outpouring of grassroots generosity, would our churches be the right recipients? In other words, would that additional money be spent on expansion of the kingdom? Or would we simply buy nicer chairs?

Most churches do not give even 10 percent of the money they collect to the poor or to causes outside their own operations.[2] The majority of the money collected, sadly, goes back into the operation of running services, during which they collect more money. We need to be liberated from this kind of financial futility. That will take both willingness and action.

Churches in the United States should be giving away large portions of their income. We are not free from the original mandate for the people of God: "There need be no poor people among you."[3] The fight against global poverty notwithstanding, there should not be poverty, homelessness, and joblessness in the church itself. Let's start with that modest proposal for change.

It is my contention that we should be spending closer to 75–100 percent of the money we collect on work that resources the mission of God in the world. This means being more generous outside the scope of our local work *and* reimagining the work we do locally. Does all the money actually go toward things that are essential to the mission? I know that matters like salary scales and amenities will be a grey area, but I think, at the very least, the question needs to be asked.

Another alternative is that we should not be collecting money at all, which is actually possible. It only seems impossible because of the cost-prohibitive structures to which we are currently indebted and because of the social pressure we feel to keep up with the cash-rich churches in our cities. If we can free ourselves from these structures, we can still run worship services and keep all the best functions of the local church, without any of the restrictions we currently experience.

Let me share a little behind-the-curtain thinking about why I have a more radical view on such things. Essentially, it's because of my experiences. I've seen this work in real-life situations—my own and others around me. I had to learn to raise money because I started out working in the parachurch ministry. We saw ourselves as missionaries in the classic sense. We did not take money from the people we were sent to serve. In my case, that was college students. Instead, we built teams of visionary donors or benefactors, who saw the value and importance of not only reaching the university, but in doing it without us having to take up offerings. These donors understood that the mission would be compromised if we had to collect money from our students in order to make our salaries or pay our expenses. Consider the wisdom of this model.

Our Platform Is Free

Missionaries, both overseas and in national parachurch organizations, have always known that they needed to find a few committed partners *before* entering the mission field so that they are free to give away the gospel without cost and also so that there would be no confusion as to the motivation of the missionary-entering culture. The parachurch has found for us a useful alternative, however, and maybe even a superior model that can and perhaps should be used and applied in new ecclesial constructions.

Parachurch itself is a misnomer. For decades, we bifurcated the church into the constructs of what Ralph Winter calls the modality and sodality of the church, an elegant kind of distribution of labor.[4] We rooted the work of the local church in the sacraments and centralized buildings. We gave the work of teaching and shepherding to these modes of churches, and, in turn, we outsourced the work of mission to the sodalities of "para" church ("para" means to come "alongside" the church). But these constructs do not come from the New Testament. They are an attempt to reconcile a church without mission and mission without the church. The church is supposed to be a place of refuge, community, and spiritual nurture, but it is also supposed to be a place of sending, with disbursements being dispensed to the needs and hunger of the world. There is no such thing, really, as "parachurch"; we are all the church, expressing ourselves in ways that we all need to both consider and integrate so that the church is no longer a schizophrenic version of itself. It seems there is a longing for both components to be reunited.

Churches are beginning to wake up to new realities of what they can do for God's mission too. They are starting to wonder why they have outsourced so much of their mission to the parachurch. Likewise, the parachurch is beginning to wake up to the reality that they are and have always been the church. They are starting to wonder why they have outsourced the sacraments to the local church. Why can't a Young Life staff baptize a kid? Or a Navigators staff member officiate the wedding of two of their students? Why can't a Youth for Christ worker serve communion? Likewise, why can't a local church across the street from a community college start a student ministry on that campus?

I am not proposing that churches simply adopt the financial model of the parachurch. I am only suggesting that this model is already a working alternative within the church. We really do suffer from a staggering lack of creativity. These two models are also not the only options we have. Missionaries understand they have to enter the culture and initiate relationships with no strings attached. This is why they always start their work by disentangling it from money. Jesus, the consummate missionary, was the ultimate free service provider.

Jesus gives his life freely. We cannot enter the kingdom except through some kind of mysterious transaction of grace. We cannot earn it or work for it, and we certainly cannot deserve it. Once that grace has become a part of us—once we are saved by it— somehow the dynamics change. Perhaps out of gratitude or loving obedience (or maybe even a supernatural compulsion now within us), we begin to live differently. If it is grace that saves us, it is, then, work that bears witness to that grace. Works do matter to

God. While they will never save us and they do not earn our place in the kingdom nor the affection of our Father, we are still commanded to walk in his ways through good works, to represent his will, and to do his work in the world—generally, to serve the purposes of his kingdom. That is what grace means; it is free and it is freely given. Yet, that free gift manifests into a relationship of love, respect, and submission.

The church is meant to mirror this dynamic: we are supposed to offer our words and service to the world for free. I think the centralized form of the church should serve the decentralized form, and it should do so for free. I say this because it has been such a joy and a blessing to experience this within the UNDERGROUND that I want everyone else to experience it too. We should do so with no strings attached, as a true demonstration of Christlikeness. This kind of platform is not just a good idea, it is an example of the gospel. We offer missionaries our time and services for free to remind them of the gospel itself. They, too, offer their love and service to the needy and the unbeliever in the city for free to remind them of the gospel. All we do should bear witness to the gospel. Thus, our secondary work should mirror the primary work of Jesus. What he did for us, we should do for others. As he said, "Now that I, your Lord and Teacher, have washed your feet, you also should wash one another's feet."[5]

In the UNDERGROUND, as I mentioned in passing above, we offer five foundational services for anyone called to lead in the kingdom. Here is exactly what they look like:

- Training, which includes the Crucible (weekend conference for missionaries), summer institute (seminary-level applied theology), written resources, open-source seminars, calling lab, elders training course, and ordination.
- Financial Services, which include banking and accounting, purchasing cards, donation processing, tax services, payroll, and basic human resources.

- Media Services, which include logo design, web design, video and print media, as well as creative consulting.
- Facilities, which include printing services, banquet room, classrooms, free clinic, auditorium, and use of all our co-op spaces for conferencing, meetings, co-working, and private offices.
- Coaching, which means every microchurch is assigned one of our trained coaches, who help leaders navigate the articulation and pursuit of their own mission, while supporting them personally and connecting them to critical resources both within and outside the UNDERGROUND.

In turn, our service to these leaders and core teams results in thoughtful, inspired leadership and service to hundreds of mission gaps in our city. Here is a list of some of the people currently served just in the city of Tampa:

Victims of the sex industry
LGBTQ+
Young black girls
Immigrants
Homeless
At-risk youth
Men and women in prison
Youth in correctional facilities
Pub regulars
College students
Artists
Pregnant women
Neighbors
Young professionals
Nurses
Healthcare workers
Individuals without insurance

Latin American community
Asian and Asian-American community
Teachers
Women
Foster children
Foster parents
Black women
Young adults
High school students
Middle school students
Sports fans
Gamers
Recovering addicts
Those who have been hurt by the church
Abuse victims
Communities impacted with disabilities
People struggling with

mental illness
Deaf community
Widows/widowers
Caregivers of children with disabilities
Haitian community
Fathers
Single parents
Formerly incarcerated
Graphic designers
Photographers
Musicians
Skate community
Dancers
Actors
Police
Those in assisted living facilities
Athletes
Refugees
Scientists

How We Do It

The UNDERGROUND offers an alternative, a third way. It might seem like a house of cards, but our financial model is built on five pillars: visionary benefactors, the commonwealth, core support, staff partner support, and radical budgeting. Again, I am not offering our strategy as an archetype, only as an alternative and a starting place for new financial systems for churches to adopt.

VISIONARY BENEFACTORS

For too long the church has been making a case for giving based on the storehouse metaphor in Malachi.[6] That is, we have likened the operations of the local church building to the temple. The problem with the analogy is based on the fact that Jesus never suggested it. Even more, the era of the temple has ended, and God's presence in the world is no longer defined by a building, but his presence extends into the world through his people. That means that we're contradicting the new covenant principle of God's presence with us. As I have already argued, the temple system called for a centripetal force: all of religious life was being drawn inward toward the temple and the house of God. His presence was somehow mysteriously contained by this structure and even more directly upon the ark of his covenant. Not only is that temple long since destroyed, but Jesus spent the majority of his ministry and life on earth replacing the temple and its system with his person and new covenantal systems. Instead, the itinerant nature of Jesus's incarnation and mission implied the opposite of centripetal—his kingdom then is centrifugal, spinning its force outward from the person of Jesus into the world. In other words, we no longer come to one place, one building, to find God. He is everywhere.

To use the metaphor of the storehouse, or even to think about the church as the new temple (house of God), is theologically irresponsible and contributes to our passivity about mission. It is inappropriate to say that people should give 10 percent of their money to their local church if that church is not in fact operating in the spirit of the kingdom.

Instead, we should have to make a case to our people as donors, benefactors, and investors in the work of mission. In this case, we may have even more accountability because every believer is keenly aware of their responsibility for stewarding all of their money in the cause of the kingdom. Still, some give more than others, and those people in particular should be considered angel investors. Since these "investors" are funding the bulk of the work, they should be considered as a kind of financial oversight committee for the mission. What I am suggesting is that we treat all givers as donors and treat these higher-level philanthropic investors with more respect, recognizing the role God has given them.

Occasionally, I have a ministry idea that requires serious money. What to do? One approach is to operate in a system that deifies all the senior leader's ideas so that they are all immediately funded by unilateral power. This is problematic, not only because of the imbalance of power (how many other people would have that kind of latitude?), but it is also a poor way to vet ideas. Surely all of that leader's ideas are not worth funding.

Another approach would be to try and raise that money. That is, to go out and leverage leadership credibility and relationships to fund the idea—to pitch or convince potentially reluctant parties to believe in or support an idea that is not their own and that they may not really believe will work. I have experienced both approaches.

The better way, in my experience, is to bring an idea to people who are gifted in philanthropy and investment. The goal is not to ask for the money, but to ask if they think the idea is worth funding at all. The members of my own team of visionary benefactors have become partners in our work. When I have a new idea, I am eager to ask them if they think the idea is from God or not. Then,

I ask them if it is the right time or not. They vote with their funding. If they will not fund the project, then I am not disappointed. Instead, I am relieved that we do not enter into something that was likely not from God.

At least in the North American context, the people who fund kingdom work should be given more input into the form and function of that work. I am not suggesting that funding should hold the missionary captive, only that the people who make it their work to give often have the expertise to ask the hard questions about execution that are a grace and a necessary filter for good ideas. If you want to see something like the UNDERGROUND in your city, you will need some of these visionary benefactors to agree to help.

COMMONWEALTH

"Commonwealth," a term that originates in the fifteenth century, is an expression of a political community that serves the public well-being. It is something held by all for the good of all. To think about the church as a commonwealth is helpful. The word that has come to mean our money (wealth) is a derivation of the English expression, "well-being." The wealth we hold in common—what was called in the early church, the common purse—is a measure of our collective financial well-being. We all have a certain amount of wealth and resources, and in the kingdom, those resources are a part of the commonwealth and should be managed accordingly.

In the UNDERGROUND, to reinforce this concept, we nurture a culture of sharing and giving. This distinction is important because we do not just "give to the church," we share all we have with the people of God. We do not give a percentage to the church with no concern or knowledge of how that money is used. We care very much how the church stewards their money. Likewise, they should care very much how we, the members of the body, steward the money we keep.

That first church was both generous and accountable. They gave when there was need. They shared their wealth, property, and resources. There was no talk of the tithe, as far as we know— just generous giving. That is important, not because the tithe is wrong, but because the tithe was being superseded. In the same way that Jesus explained that he had not come to abolish the Law but to fulfill it, so too the first church realized that Jesus had not come to abolish the tithe but to fulfill it. We are asking everyone to see their whole lives, their relationships, dreams, gifts, possessions, and, yes, their money as the possession of God and as a part of the commonwealth of his people. This ensures we remember that we all must steward all we have and that we should, therefore, make it available to the needs of the people of God and his kingdom. We do not ask for a tithe at the UNDERGROUND; we ask for a surrendered life. The result is that our people make less and give more. They give directly and indirectly to the mission work they do, and they also give to the collective work, which makes possible the generosity of the UNDERGROUND as a whole.

All the money given is used for mission. Half of it goes toward the infrastructure of the UNDERGROUND, and the other half is distributed to our microchurches and to other missionary work around the world. Giving aside, for us at the UNDERGROUND, an equally radical commitment to share allows us to do more with less. We maintain a strange and beautiful expectation of simplicity in our lives that has created a culture in which our people do not feel pressure to build great personal wealth or to live in luxury. To that they add their willingness to share the small pieces of wealth they do have—whether trucks or tools or any kind of possession that we all need from time to time. This, too, is part of how we do what we do.

CORE COMMITMENTS

Years ago, I served as an unpaid member of the leadership team for a medium-size traditional church. One hurricane season, we were hearing reports that a category 4 hurricane might hit us over the weekend. The question was posed, "What should we do? Should we still hold services?" I was bewildered. "Are you guys serious? Just cancel it," I said.

Everyone got quiet. People were shifting in their seats like there was some awkward reality everyone knew but me. Finally, the executive pastor explained, "We need that offering, Brian." In that moment, I got a crash course in the economics of offerings. You see, the safety of our people aside, losing one Sunday meant losing one offering, which for them was about $20,000. That was money that would not be recovered. This was the model they were managing. They needed to pass those plates in order to collect money. They were not in a committed relationship with their donors; they were running a show, and you don't pay for the movie you don't see—that's the reality that hit me squarely in the face that day.

When the economic model is tied to the Sunday service, there seems to be an implication that the money is given *for* the worship service. It is payment for services rendered, not support for the work and mission of the church. Surely there were people who saw it differently, but that was the implicit message of the model they were using at that church, which enslaved them to the weekend service for the flow of funds.

I never wanted to find myself in that place again. Instead, at the UNDERGROUND, we have tried to treat our people as valued donors. We ask them directly to pledge and then gently hold them to their commitment. But what ties it all together, in my opinion, is a sacrificial life and committed relationships. With a Sunday show model, the relationships are often what is missing the most. The kingdom cannot advance without covenant between people of virtue. Our model is tied to committed relationships and personal integrity.

In *Nicomachean Ethics*, Aristotle reasoned that there were three levels of friendship: the first level was friendship based on *utility.* People relate to each other at times because they are useful to each other in some way. The second level of friendship, he said, was based on *pleasure.* Sometimes people enjoy each other and share their lives because it is pleasurable to do so. They simply enjoy each other's company. But the highest level of friendship, Aristotle argued, was a friendship based on *virtue.* These relation ships are formed by people who are drawn together by their common will to be better and to hold each other to some ideal of goodness.

While I do think that the amount of money people choose to give should be private, I think we gain a certain fortitude when we give in view of one another. The level of our sacrifice is something that should be between the giver and God, but the idea that we are all committed is something that helps us to give. We all commit something; we all make our stand so that we all feel that solidarity and communal strength. Our collective commitment endows our meager gift with greater meaning and challenges all of us to "remember the poor" and to grow in the grace of giving.[7]

When thinking over the financial challenges, we came up with the idea that once a year we would gather all of our core people—those who felt especially connected and committed to the UNDERGROUND—and ask them to commit to the common budget of the community. We usually set a goal for the year and lay out an organizational budget for them to see. We have an open time of dialogue about that budget and then ask each committed person to decide what they will give. Those pledges, then, become the operating budget for the year. In other words, we ask them what they plan to give, and that is what we know we will have to spend. We are not raising money; we are stewarding it in the service of the community and mission of God. Whatever they pledge is what we have to spend in their name, and for Jesus's sake.

This frees us from the tyranny of offerings and the dependency on worship services. Even though we now offer a Sunday-morning gathering to our people, we do not need all of them to use that service (in fact, most of them don't). One of the perks of this financial model is that we are free to cancel Sunday service at any time. We take five or six Sundays off every year for various reasons (sometimes just because we want to take a break). We do not need a "giving" sermon before every offering, and we do not even need to talk about money with our people outside of the annual gathering. We rely on their verbal commitment once a year to give us a picture of what we have to work with. Then, we plan accordingly.

STAFF PARTNER SUPPORT

Because we need to be generous with the money these missionaries commit, we are in turn committed to giving at least half of it away through grants that support the work of organizations and entities outside of our 501(c)3. We are committed to partners all over the world. Since our facility is also a major gift we give to all our local microchurches, a good portion of the remaining 50 percent is designated for that service. This leaves precious little to pay the salaries necessary to lead and operate the infrastructure we have created. In Tampa alone, at the time of writing, we have seventeen staff members. This means that our staff, who are also missionaries, have to raise personal support.

If you understand the process of support raising for overseas and parachurch missionaries, then you have an idea of what our staff do. We do not charge any overhead, and in most cases, we augment their salary with some money from the common purse budget and our visionary patrons. Still, many of us raise the entirety of our support as a show of solidarity with the missionaries who make up the network (some of whom raise money and most of whom are bivocational).

We need our staff to take on the work of raising money because we believe so deeply not only in our own work, but in the work we make possible. This is congruent with the culture of giving, sharing, and sacrifice that courses through the blood of the whole organization.

RADICAL BUDGETS

All this means there is simply no room for waste. Not only is the money always *by design* going to be tight, but we now carry a public trust with our people and with the cities where we serve. This means we cannot be frivolous with the money we do collect and we are bound by a missionary's tastes and sensibilities about what being frivolous means. Our commitment to the poor, for instance, means we have to always be asking ourselves, *Is this expense necessary for us to accomplish our mission? Will it serve all the microchurches?* If not, we know that we could give it to the poor directly. If you visit our facilities, you will see there is almost no flooring, rarely drop ceilings, and precious few amenities. Our choice to purchase 500 mismatched used theater chairs for $2 each, for example, saved us about $25,000. We gave away the money we would have spent on nice, new chairs instead. The chairs we bought work just as well as new ones. Buying used is one example of spending that creates a kind of ethos that reinforces our values. It is not that we are unwilling to spend money, only that it is done with the healthy accountability of our people who often make very little but sacrifice a lot. We know that the money we collect comes from sacrificial people, and if they saw us wasting money on exorbitant salaries, elaborate meals, unnecessary travel, and superfluous amenities, they might lose faith in us organizationally.

Wanting a radical community and the culture I have described in this book is deeply related to this kind of fiscal responsibility. If you want these kinds of people to be a part of your church, you have to spend money differently. I'm not saying every church should live in this way; God calls some communities one way and others in other ways. This, we believe, is how we're being faithful to God's call on us. I write this simply to present an alternative to what many churches do as a way of offering hope for those who want to live like this.

Here is a depiction of the expenditures by percentage for the most recent year. There has been very little fluctuation of these percentages over the years. While I would not present this model as a financial rule, I would point to this budget allocation as an example of what it can look like when a church restructures and repositions its money for mission.

The budgets will need to be as radical as we are, because our budgets are one of the truest reflections of our hearts, our values, and our commitment. We cannot be afraid to collect and spend money; that has been a part of the practice of the church since its inception. But we do need to reconsider how we collect and spend money if we are looking for a more potent expression of the church. To change everything else we have talked about while leaving our money untouched would almost certainly sabotage the highest hopes. "Where your treasure is," Jesus said, "there your heart will be also."[8]

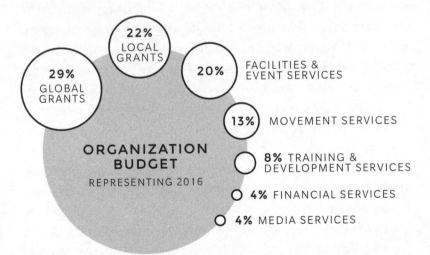

WINDOW 3

The UNDERGROUND HUB is buzzing. I am running late to the next session at our annual gathering called "Core Conference." As I finish a deep reconnect with Jason, the director of our sister movement in Germany, I can hear music from our makeshift auditorium. I'm anxious to get in there, because I don't want to miss a minute of it.

I squeeze through the side doors and start to make my way through the crowd to the back of the room. I like to sit in the back—partly because I prefer to be unseen, and partly because I love watching these people worship. Almost everyone in the UNDERGROUND comes to this gathering, so we have people in the room who have been with us from the start, but we also have people who have only recently joined the network. There are even people who use our services but will only come to one or two events a year. No one is the same; still, they all seem to treasure this moment. They all are experiencing some kind of relief at being together.

I will be preaching soon, so I sit down and try to focus. The music is strong, alive. The multiethnic team of musicians leads a multinational audience. I have walked into something that is both new and old, something living and ancient, like a river of awe and fascination that flows from the throne of God through time to this moment. It's the beauty of the body of Christ fully alive, the face of Jesus among his people. I try to remember my prophet's mandate for that day, the word that I will carry like a burden until it's delivered. But I am distracted.

I see Simon and his team from Ireland, Taylor and his people from Birmingham, and the Filipinos all sitting near me. Some of those are the same Filipino leaders I met all those years ago. I think about those first days, when we went to them for life and leadership. Now they are here with us, a part of this movement that God has willed into the world.

The room is packed, and in moments like this, filled as it is, the sound of the community rises above the sound system. This, too, seems supernatural. The missionaries raise their voices, their hands, their hearts, and their courage to God. Jesus is here—again—and again, I break down. I am distracted by the grandeur of it all—of how far we have come and how our community has shown that simple things, when taken together, are indomitable.

It's my turn now. I get up to pour myself out. Preaching to this group is different than preaching in other contexts. They are so hungry, so faithful, so humble, and yet so fierce. I say something about dreaming big and living small. I say something about how their courage and faithfulness pleases God. I tell them not to give up. I tell them there is still more to do. I ask them for more, for greater works than these.

As I close, I can see the table we have set up just below the stage. It has a giant copy of our leadership covenant on it. I finish by calling on our leaders to come forward and sign it again—to pledge in plain sight and to put their name to the standard we all know we need. From that same vantage point, I watch hundreds of them stream forward, one after another. Saying "Yes" again.

Our "yes" to them has been important, but it is nothing compared to their "yes" to God. It is their "yes" to that yearning, that calling to the poor, to the margins, to the weak, and to the unbelieving that makes us what we are. It is his work in them that I celebrate in this moment. I celebrate, too, the spectacle of watching ordinary people exercise extraordinary faith. Again, I try to hold it together. I am not an overly emotional person. I rarely cry, but the Holy Spirit and this strange missionary community have changed that. They have changed me. They have brought me back to life and have taught me to hope again. I don't think anyone knows the flaws of the UNDERGROUND as well as I do. I see that, too, and still, it is a miracle. They are a miracle, and so I do the only sane thing a person can do when they witness a miracle. Through tears and laughter, I worship him.

A BRAVE FUTURE

*We must learn to reawaken and keep
ourselves awake, not by mechanical aid, but
by an infinite expectation of the dawn.*

HENRY DAVID THOREAU

I think the UNDERGROUND is a little bit like Netscape Navigator. Remember that revolutionary, clunky, buggy web browser by that name? We are like that too, at least I hope we will be considered like it one day. Netscape Navigator was a new interface on a new frontier. It was not the best and certainly not the last, but it started the ball of innovation rolling. No one uses Netscape anymore; it has been replaced by better, more elegant alternatives. I hold the same hope for our form of church. Maybe the UNDERGROUND will be remembered as something that started us thinking about church in a new way, and maybe you and your community will be the ones to find even better ways to see the church in its fullness, in our time.

Since what our hearts most yearn for is the coming of that inevitable kingdom, we are all equally pleased or, as my grandmother would have said, "tickled" for someone else to come along and do it better. In fact, I am counting on it. Maybe you are the person I'm counting on and your community is the community that will find a way to build upon the results of our field research—to do it even better. I certainly hope so. I always encourage people by telling them that starting something is enough. It pleases God to try. The hardest growth is from zero to one. Trying requires real courage. Only the brave can forcefully advance the kingdom, so don't be afraid.

God Is Almost Never Where You Saw Him Last

When I spend any amount of time staring across a body of water, it is the vastness, the uniformity that is most therapeutic for me. Sitting on the ocean shore is a way of calming my mind because it seems endless and yet so calm. Although I know that there is a world of life teeming beneath the surface, it is all out of sight and out of mind to me. Until, that is, something extraordinary happens and a creature from beneath the surface breaks into my world above the surface. Where I live in Florida, we get the occasional dolphin sighting as they come up for air or as they just enjoy the play of breaking the surface. When they do this, it commands your whole attention.

Maybe it is the simple juxtaposition of this one mysterious creature breaking the spell of all that vastness that is breathtaking. When it happens, it happens fast and their waves disappear as quickly as they appeared. Suddenly, you want nothing more than to see it happen again, and so you stare—usually where you saw them last. But that is a mistake. Although I know that dolphins are creatures of perpetual motion, and although I know that the one place they certainly will *not* appear is where I last saw them, still, that is where I am tempted to look.

I think God might be a little bit like the appearance of dolphins, and our anticipation of his movements are like my eyes on the waters of the ocean. We have an almost involuntary urge to look for God where we last saw him, to memorialize him and wait for him there, not realizing that God is always moving. All we know for sure is that if we hope to see him again, we have to acknowledge that he is always on the move.

One of the more peculiar moments in the New Testament is the ascension. Not just because of the presence of talking angels or a levitation of Jesus, but because of what is said afterward. Jesus leaves his friends with some last words, words of promise and commission, and then literally ascends into the clouds before their eyes. Having been students in the school of miracles, this one has to be the most bewildering. So, as he disappears into the clouds, they are, predictably and understandably, mouths agape, staring into the sky. They are looking for Jesus where they last saw him—naturally. But the angels don't seem so understanding. Their response is, "Men of Galilee . . . why do you stand here looking into the sky?"[1] Really? The answer isn't obvious?

He will return, but not right here and not right now. In fact, he will come with the clouds, so keep your eyes up. But the one place you can be sure he will *not* return is right here right now.

My point is this: we have created church structures throughout history for purposes that make sense at the time. It's usually the best we can do given our resources, background, and context. Then, new structures and systems come along with new eras. It isn't that old systems are bad or wrong. Yes, some may be "off," but that is to miss the point and purpose of change with the mission and self-definition of the church. We should neither memorialize nor vilify the old systems of the church. Assuming that they were very good, at least for a time, and a means of grace for the people of God, does it mean that they were meant for longer than one moment in time and space? We easily forget that God is moving, that the nature of God defies nature itself. To be confined by natural process, laws, or any predictable system is to be mastered by it. The creator cannot be contained by the created world. He can no more be conjured by a rote prayer than he can by a deck of cards or a crystal ball.

God is free, autonomous, and transcendent. So it is our quest to find him, know him, and catch occasional glimpses of him. On this quest, we would do well to remember that he will only be found by us if he wants to be found and that he will appear when and where he pleases to be seen. So our eyes must scan the horizon of our lives, of mission, of the hurting world. We will not find the new ways of his grace in our institutions because institutions are, by definition, old. God is younger by far. If there is a purpose for institutions, it should be to preserve and protect this truth, to hold on to the unchanging truth that Jesus calls people to follow him and that only the surrendered heart will be able to keep up. We cannot trust in the old paths any more than we can trust in the new ones. We must instead keep growing and learning and nurture our hunger for God. Through this, we will see him appear more often than in our organizational processes.

This is just the first chapter of the UNDERGROUND story. For all I know, it will become a cautionary tale. If it does, that too will be worth telling, because it is in our stories—in our reflection of the past—that we find our way forward. But of this much I am sure, if we are not willing to change, we will not see God again.

The irony here is that to capture the glory of some previous generation we must refuse to be exactly like them. We honor their encounter with the moving God by embracing change and finding him in our unique time and space. This takes tremendous courage for every generation.

The future of the church is tied to the bravery of its people. If we will not rekindle the fire of Jesus and his kingdom in our own hearts and let it burn out of control, we will be resigned to living as a people whose best days are behind us. I do not claim to fully understand the plan that God has for this world or exactly how it will all play out; I do not know if things must get worse before the kingdom comes, or if they will steadily get better; I do not know if we will find ourselves in an increasingly futile battle or if we will see his reign and rule take shape. What I do know is that we are called and expected by a living God to join him in his redemption of this place in which we live. We are somehow a part of this cosmic history being written.

I am convinced that the lamb's book of life is actually a story and that to have your name written in it does not mean you made the list, but that you played a role in the narrative of his coming kingdom. I do know that one day we will be made into a kingdom of priests to rule and reign with him. Even on that day when he left his disciples and ascended into heaven, the promise of his return was accompanied by the conferring of this kingdom. He gave his friends and followers the keys and the heart of this kingdom on that day. Every day that has since followed, every day I wake into this terrifying and beautiful world, that kingdom is also mine to know and live. And it is yours. Now we see in part, Paul wrote, but one day, all of this labor and all of this love will be proved to be the very best things we did with our lives.

Still, it is our fear that threatens us. The kingdom will come. He has promised it and its consummation as sure as the sun that rises each day. But our part in it is still yet to be written. Although I know that my salvation is secure, what is left uncertain is my participation in the coming of Jesus and his kingdom.

So I urge you to live the way the apostle Peter wrote, so as to speed his coming. Live without fear.

So, I leave you with the haunting question that Sheryl Sandberg asks in her important book, *Lean In*, "What would you do if you were not afraid?" If you can answer that question, in the presence of Jesus, you are on your way to not only a new way of doing church, but to taking part in the transformation of the world.

Behold, he is making all things new: new wine, new wineskins, a new heaven, a new earth, a new covenant, a new command, a new Jerusalem, and you, a new creation. The work of God is always renewal. Don't be afraid.

THE MANIFESTO

1. **Jesus.** The way of Jesus is our way. Before and in all things, we value Jesus as the image of the invisible God. We long to worship Jesus by imitating his life and ministry. Both our theology and praxis is relentlessly Christological. He is our model, mentor, hero, mediator, savior, judge, king, and ruler of all. All of our values flow from what we understand about his character, concerns, and the practices of his ministry (Matthew 28:19, John 1:3, John 13:15, John 14:6, John 17:18, Romans 5:10, Ephesians 1:22–23, Philippians 2:5, Colossians 1:15–20, Colossians 2:9, Colossians 3:17, Hebrews 1:3, Hebrews 12:2, [MODEL] Ephesians 5:1–2, [MENTOR] John 13:14–15, Acts 26:16, [HERO] Romans 1:4, [MEDIATOR] 1 Timothy 2:5, Hebrews 7:25, [SAVIOR] Acts 4:12, Titus 3:6, [JUDGE] Romans 2:16, John 9:39, 2 Timothy 4:1, [KING] Revelation 1:5, Revelation 19:16, [RULER OF ALL] Colossians 1:18, Revelation 17:14).

2. **The Poor.** We will remember the poor because we believe that God does. We believe that they are central to his mission in the world. It is our conviction that God is always on the side of those who have no one on their side. For that reason, we believe the church should also stand on the side of the poor, and in so doing, stand in solidarity with the heart and work of God. Jesus's own ministry is our model. We welcome all people but prioritize the poor in our ministry concern, allocation of resources, and advocacy. We do this, not because

the rich and middle class are less important to God, but because they already have access to resources and are able to advocate their own cause. It is our belief that the church should therefore prioritize and remember those who have less, and access to less, so that in all things there might be equality (Deuteronomy 15:7, Deuteronomy 15:11, Psalm 82:3, Psalm 140:12, Proverbs 14:31, Isaiah 61:1, Jeremiah 8:21, Jeremiah 22:16, Matthew 11:5, Matthew 25:40, Mark 2:17, Luke 4:18, Luke 6:20, Luke 7:22, Luke 14:23, Luke 18:22, 2 Corinthians 8:9, 13, Galatians 2:10).

3. **The Lost.** We value lost people because they are spiritually poor. We believe the good news of the kingdom is the most important commodity with which the church and the people of God have been entrusted. For this reason, we will engage the lost. We believe that the church should not expect lost people to come and find them, but that we are called and sent to "seek and save that which was lost." Again, we will emphasize the life and ministry of Jesus by prioritizing those who have not yet heard and believed the good news. This is our first and most important task, even in our ministry to the poor and the lost (who could be considered the spiritually poor). They are our first concern (Genesis 22:17–18, Matthew 4:23, Matthew 10:7, Matthew 18:14, Matthew 28:19, Mark 13:10, Luke 15:4, 6, Luke 19:10, Luke 24:46–47, Acts 1:8, Acts 10:42, Romans 10:14–15, Romans 15:20, Galatians 2:10).

4. **The Whole World.** While we understand that our most transforming ministry will take place where we are planted and in our own city, we commit ourselves to the mission of God to reach the whole world. We believe that Jesus came as the savior, not of one people, but of the whole world. We value the world because we believe that God is a global God. We assume responsibility for the world, not because we believe we

can reach it alone, but because we accept the mandate of the great commission and the heart of God to love and sacrifice for the discipleship of the whole world. We accept this apostolic mandate to send and be sent into every part of the world, and our place in partnership with the global church (Psalm 22:7, Psalm 24:1, Isaiah 41:9, Matthew 24:14, Mark 16:15, John 1:29, John 3:16–17, John 4:42, John 6:33, John 6:51, John 8:12, John 12:46–47, John 17:21, Romans 5:18, 2 Corinthians 5:19, 1 John 2:2, 1 John 4:14, Revelation 14:6).

5. **Culture and Ethnicity.** Similarly, we affirm that every culture and ethnicity, while imperfect, reflects the mosaic of God's own image, and together we better glorify and serve the God of creation. We value every people, language, and culture in our city and in the world. We believe that the church of Jesus Christ was meant to demonstrate the power of the gospel through reconciliation, unity, and the beauty of a multiethnic community. For that reason, we do not just admire multiethnic communities, but purpose to become one. We do not believe in being color-blind. Rather, we hope to accept and include the beauty and wisdom of every culture in our city and in our communities (Genesis 1:27, Psalm 67:2–3, Isaiah 56:7, Daniel 7:13–14, Joel 2:28, Haggai 2:7, Malachi 1:11, John 17:20–22, Acts 10:34–35, Acts 17:26–27, Romans 14:11, Romans 15:5, 6, 1 Corinthians 12:12–14, Ephesians 2:14–22, Philippians 2:10–11, Revelation 5:9–10, Revelation 7:9, Revelation 14:6).

6. **Contextualization.** We will not trust in franchising or empire-building through paradigm propagation. Rather, we will value the empowerment of every microchurch community to contextualize the proclamation and demonstration of the gospel to the people they hope to reach. Our paradigm is that there is no one paradigm. We believe in contextualized structures with revolutionary content. Learning from the ministry of Jesus, we will not try to

bring surface transformation (to culture or structures), but rather will contextualize our structures to what people can and will understand, so that the revolutionary message of the kingdom and the liberating work of the Holy Spirit will be received (John 1:14, Acts 16:3, Acts 17:22–23, Romans 12:2, 1 Corinthians 3:5–9, 1 Corinthians 9:19–23, 1 Corinthians 10:32–33, Philippians 2:5–8, [the passages of the ministry of Jesus and his parables are all examples of contextualization]).

7. **Zeal and Contemplation.** We will value the paradox of exuberance and zeal in worship, community life, and evangelism, while at the same time wholeheartedly pursuing the rhythm and profound importance of silence and solitude for personal contemplation and rest. We affirm seasons of zeal and charismatic expression of the greatness and majesty of God along with seasons of silence and stillness before God. We value each, and both together. We hope for a fusion of the two in a life of zeal, lived ablaze and unashamed for God, and contemplation, lived in deep awareness and quiet appreciation for God ([ZEAL] Psalm 47:5, Psalm 98:4, Isaiah 42:13, Matthew 11:28–28, Matthew 17:5, Mark 6:31, John 10:27, Romans 12:11, Titus 2:14, [CONTEMPLATION] Psalm 46:10, Psalm 48:9, Psalm 95:6, 2 Corinthians 3:18, Colossians 3:2, 1 Peter 1:13).

8. **Simplicity.** We commit to live a life free from clutter and the allure of materialism. We affirm that every believer and every community of believers has a responsibility to renounce the sins of its own people. As North Americans, we renounce the slavery and idolatry of materialism by embracing a simple lifestyle. We do not believe that money or things are in themselves evil or to be avoided, but that the love of money and things is one of the greatest perils facing Western Christianity in our time. We willingly use material things and wealth for the service of the kingdom, but not for personal

fulfillment or inappropriate luxury. In so doing, we again value the poor who have less, justice in living for equality, and personal holiness in pursuing a wholehearted devotion to God (Ecclesiastes 5:10, Matthew 6:19, 24, 26, Matthew 10:10, Mark 4:19, Mark 12:43, Luke 9:3, Luke 12:15, 33, 1 Timothy 6:7, Hebrews 13:5).

9. **Sharing and Giving.** Because we value community and simplicity, we commit ourselves to both sharing and giving. We will share because it promotes relationship and breaks the bondage of possessiveness. We believe the Western doctrine of personal property is imperfect and needs to be tempered with the more biblical value of generosity and sacrifice. In sharing what we have with others, we confess that God is the true owner and that we are only stewards in his vineyard. We will also give, because in giving, we destroy the grip of materialism over our hearts because we release the resource, wealth, or possession completely into the control of another. For that reason, we will pursue relentless generosity and the holding of all things in common. For this reason, we encourage our people to give as often and as generously as they can, and to consider themselves stewards of the rest. Likewise, the collective finances of the church and ministries should set an example in this regard (Malachi 3:10, Matthew 25:40, Luke 3:11, Acts 2:43, Acts 4:32, Acts 20:35, 2 Corinthians 8:7, 2 Corinthians 9:10–13, 2 Corinthians 8:13, Ephesians 4:28, 1 Thessalonians 2:8, 1 Timothy 6:18, 1 John 3:17).

10. **Each Other.** We commit ourselves to each other. We believe that God calls us into his mission together, never alone. We value mission and ministry done in community. We believe that God did not intend for us to be alone, and that isolation, fear of each other, and spiritual competition are cancers in the church. We believe that moral and theological failures,

controlling leadership, and many of our emotional struggles stem from a lack of community. We value free, committed, and loving friendship. Whenever possible, we will lead through teams and the sharing of life at every level with trusted friends who are an extension of the grace and presence of God in our lives (Ecclesiastes 4:9–10, Matthew 18:20, John 15:13, Acts 2:44, Romans 12:4–8, 10, Romans 13:8, Romans 15:7, 1 Corinthians 10:24, Galatians 6:2, Ephesians 4:11–13, Ephesians 5:21, Philippians 2:3–4, Hebrews 3:15, Hebrews 10:24–25, Hebrews 6:10–11, 1 Peter 3:8, 1 John 3:16, 7–12, Revelation 4:4, 10).

11. **Kingdom Mission.** We will do mission because we are sent people. We believe that the church is not the church until it is engaged in the mission for which God has called it into his marvelous light. We crave healing, discipleship, and intimacy with God. But we believe that all of these things come in large part through obedience to the mission. We believe that healing comes through offering healing to others, that discipleship does not primarily take place in a lecture but through doing. We believe that intimacy with God comes from being in his presence and through submission to his will, by doing what he is doing. Since we believe that the life of Jesus and the early church demonstrate that God himself is with the lost and the poor of the earth, proclaiming the good news of his kingdom, we also believe that when we co-labor with him as workers in that harvest field, we not only bring the kingdom into that place, but that we also experience the deepest and truest intimacy with God (Psalm 51:10–13, Isaiah 58:6–8, Matthew 9:35–38, Matthew 25:40, Matthew 28:18–20, Mark 1:14–15, 38, Luke 4:18–21, John 4:34, 35, John 6:27, John 9:4, John 12:26, John 15:9–10, John 17:18, Acts 1:8, Romans 15:20, 1 Corinthians 15:58, 2 Corinthians 5:18–19, Ephesians 2:10, Philippians 2:3, Colossians 3:17, 23, 1 John 3:18, 1 Peter 2:9).

12. **Humility.** We commit to pursue humility as one of the chief virtues. We expect it in leadership, in community and relationships, in our theology, in the contextualization of our mission, in our prayer, and even in our appraisal of ourselves and others. We are convinced that humility is necessary for following Jesus as an individual and as an organization. In individuals, we hope for humility in all our relationships and leadership roles. As an organization, we hope to be flexible, looking always to refine our commitments and to expand our understanding and revelation of God and his call upon us. We believe in the living prophetic Word of God, that it can be heard and obeyed, yet we also believe that we are flawed listeners and should always listen and follow with humility (Psalm 25:9, Psalm 51:17, Psalm 147:6, Psalm 149:4, Proverbs 11:2, Proverbs 18:12, Proverbs 22:4, Ecclesiastes 5:2, Isaiah 29:19, Isaiah 57:15, Isaiah 66:2, Micah 6:8, Matthew 5:3, Matthew 11:29, Matthew 18:3–4, Matthew 20:26, Matthew 23:12, Luke 1:52, Luke 6:20, Luke 10:21, Luke 14:10, Luke 17:10, Luke 18:13–14, Luke 22:26–27, John 13:14, Romans 10, Romans 11:20, Romans 12:3, Romans 16, 1 Corinthians 1:28, 1 Corinthians 3:18, 1 Corinthians 10:12, 1 Corinthians 13:4, 2 Corinthians 11:30, 2 Corinthians 12:6, 2 Corinthians 10, Galatians 5:26, Galatians 6:14, Ephesians 4:2, Philippians 2:3–11, Colossians 3:12, James 1:9, James 3:1, James 4:6, 1 Peter 3:8, 1 Peter 5:5–6).

13. **Biblical Justice.** We will live for the biblical concept of justice. We have to take a prophetic stand against all kinds of evil, not only spiritual, but also societal. All sin and injustice is the enemy of the church and the kingdom of God. The search for the kingdom of God is also a search for justice. They are the same longing. In the kingdom, we find ultimate justice, and biblical justice is more than just punishment for wrongdoing and oppression, it is also the restoration of wholeness, equality,

and peace between people and with God. Our value of justice is a call to seek the welfare of every person in our city and in the world that we can influence. It is to hope and work for the kingdom of God to come to bear on the place where we are. For that reason, our value of justice will mean action in the places where we have power, as well as the pursuit of justice in the proclamation of the kingdom wherever we have voice (Psalm 9:8, Psalm 96:10, Proverbs 31:9, Isaiah 1:15–17, Isaiah 56:1, Jeremiah 29:7, Ezekiel 34:16, Hosea 12:6, Amos 5:15, 24, Micah 6:8, Matthew 5:6, Matthew 6:10, Matthew 6:33, Matthew 12:18, Matthew 18:5, Matthew 25:40, Luke 11:42, Luke 18:7–8, Luke 19:8–10, John 2:14–17, Acts 6:1–6, Ephesians 6:12, James 1:27, 1 John 3:17, 18).

14. **Passion.** With Jesus as our model, we want our lives to be characterized by passion. In the most surface sense, this means that we should be moved by our relationship with God and maintain a high level of dedication in all we do for him. In a deeper sense, it means that we value suffering and sacrifice. We see Jesus's willingness to suffer for the lost and the hopeless as a model for all who would come after him, and that we likewise are to take up our cross and to walk the way of suffering. Not seeking pain or persecution, but not shrinking from it either. We are convinced that the clearest expression of the gospel is love, and that love is forever redefined by Jesus in his death for us. We value the kind of radical faith that expects every believer to be ready and willing to suffer and sacrifice for Jesus, his name, and his kingdom. We realize that this value is not mainstream and that it contradicts the cultural current of prosperity and the idea that in all things God wants to give us personal success. We denounce this idea and affirm that the kingdom will not be built through selfish ambition, but through passionate, sacrificial love (Psalms 63:1, Matthew 10:22, Matthew 16:24–25,

Matthew 26:38–39, Romans 5:3, Romans 8:18, Luke 9:61–62, Luke 14:27, Romans 12:1–2, 2 Corinthians 1:5, Ephesians 5:1–2, Philippians 2:3, Philippians 3:10, Colossians 1:24, Colossians 3:17, 23, 2 Timothy 2:3, 2 Timothy 3:12–15, 1 Peter 3:17, 1 John 3:16).

15. **Prayer and Dependence on God.** We commit ourselves to live a life of prayer because we believe that only God can accomplish what he calls us to do and that God should receive the glory. For this reason, we believe the church should be committed to night and day pray for the world, the coming of the kingdom, and a deeper revelation of God. Without prayer and dependence on God for all things, we are destined to either fail or become conceited in our success. We value constant prayer because we desire to know God, to deepen our understanding and revelation of his love for us and the world. We value prayer because we believe we are all called to the ministry of intercession and we want to see his kingdom come. We believe that can only happen if we ask the Lord of the harvest to send us and other laborers into the harvest field (2 Chronicles 7:14, Ezra 8:23, Psalm 17:6, Psalm 91:1–2, Isaiah 26:9, Jeremiah 29:12, Matthew 6:9–13, Matthew 6:33, Matthew 9:38, Mark 1:35, Luke 11:9–13, Luke 18:1, 7, Acts 2:42, Acts 6:4, 2 Corinthians 3:5–6, Ephesians 6:18, Philippians 4:6, Colossians 4:2, 1 Thessalonians 5:17, 1 Timothy 2:1–2, Hebrews 5:7, James 5:13–16, 1 Peter 4:7, Jude 20).

16. **Microchurches.** We affirm microchurch as the most basic expression of the church and, therefore, our ecclesiology is simple. When believers work together in sincere worship and genuine community to accomplish a part of the mission of God, they are the church. Worship, community, and mission then are the ecclesial minimum. We encourage biblically appointed leadership, sacramental worship, the pursuit of

the gifts of the Spirit, and giving, but these are desired and not required to be considered a microchurch. We believe that these churches also need the larger network, leadership, and resources of a city-wide church to strengthen, empower, and help direct the microchurch expression. We gather for worship, training, and as leadership primarily to strengthen and supply the microchurches in their labor to obey Jesus and proclaim the good news of the Kingdom to their mission field. We believe the larger church expression exists to serve the smaller, and not the other way around (Matthew 28:19–20, Luke 10:1, John 4:23, Acts 2:42–47, Acts 4:24, 31, Acts 6:3–4, 6, Acts 14:23, Acts 16:4–5, Acts 20:20, Romans 15:5–6, Romans 16:3–5, 1 Corinthians 3:16, 2 Corinthians 5:18–20, 1 Corinthians 14:26, 1 Corinthians 16:19, 2 Corinthians 3:5–61, Ephesians 2:22, Ephesians 4:16, Colossians 3:16, Colossians 4:15, Timothy 3: 2–7, Hebrews 6:10–11, Hebrews 10:24–25, 1 Peter 2:5, 9, Revelation 1:6).

17. **The Bible.** We trust the authority, reliability, and truth of all Scripture. In humility, we acknowledge we do not fully understand God and the world he made. For that reason, we rely on the Bible to be the rule of our faith, teaching us what we do not know, challenging and leading us away from our misconceptions, self-deceptions, and convenient ideas about life and God. We don't choose the parts of the Bible we prefer or want to believe, obey, or understand; instead, we submit to all of Scripture, believing it reveals the truth that is beyond us. We believe that Jesus is the Word of God, and for that reason we don't just obey Scripture, we love it. Because, like a mirror, it shows us who we really are, and like a window, it opens our lives to the beauty, wonder, and love of the God we long to know (Deuteronomy 4:10, 2 Samuel 7:28, 2 Samuel 22:31, Nehemiah 8, Psalm 18:30, Proverb 30:5, Isaiah 40:8,

Jeremiah 15:16, Matthew 4:4, Matthew 22:29, Luke 8:21, Luke 11:28, Luke 24:32, John 1:1–17, John 5:24, John 5:39, John 8:51, Acts 8:35, Acts 18:11, Romans 3:2, 1 Timothy 4:13, 2 Timothy 3:16, Colossians 1:25, Colossians 3:16, 1 Thessalonians 2:13, Hebrews 4:12–13, 1 Peter 4:11, 2 Peter 3:16, 1 John 2:5, Revelation 3:8, Revelation 19:9).

18. **Empowerment.** We affirm the priesthood of all believers. We affirm that each person who has given their life in surrender to Jesus and his cause has a unique calling from Jesus to fulfill in mission and in the church. We believe that this is only possible by the Spirit of God living in and working through each and every believer. It is the Spirit of God that empowers. Therefore, we work toward empowering each and every believer to hear and fulfill the calling of Jesus on their life. This value of empowerment is expressed in all spiritual gifts and callings for all people regardless of race, gender, or age, for the sake of Jesus's mission and for the equipping of all believers toward their maturity (Matthew 4:18–20, Matthew 10:1–15, Mark 6:7–13, Luke 4:18–19, Luke 6:12–16, Luke 11:13, John 14:26–27, John 15:1–4, John 15:26–27, John 20:22, Acts 2:1–4, Acts 4:29–31, Acts 6:3, Romans 8:9–11, Romans 8:15–17, Romans 12:3–8, 1 Corinthians 2:4–5, 1 Corinthians 2:9–16, 1 Corinthians 12, 1 Corinthians 14:1, 1 Corinthians 16:19, Galatians 5:22–26, Ephesians 4:11–13, Ephesians 4:10, 1 Timothy 1:18–19, 2 Timothy 1:7, 2 Timothy 4:19, James 4:10, 1 Peter 2:9–10, Jude 20–21, Revelation 1:5–6).

The Sum. The sum of the whole is greater than its parts. Like the people that make up the church, its commitments and values are able to *do* more in the world when they are all present in the same space.

This is a call for the church to arise, to hold on to all of these and not just a few, or the ones that are en vogue or convenient. There are more values in the Bible, but these represent the radical face of a transformed and transforming church that will take its place as the ambassadors of God and the emissaries of the kingdom that is to come and that is at hand.

NOTES

INTRODUCTION

1. Steven Johnson, "The Genius of the Tinkerer: The Secret to Innovation Is Combining Odds and Ends," *The Wall Street Journal*, September 25, 2010, https://www.wsj.com/articles/SB10001424052 748703989304575503730101860838.
2. Ibid.
3. C. S. Lewis, *The Screwtape Letters* (Glasgow: Collins, 1977), 49.
4. Matt. 9:37.

CHAPTER 1

1. Rom. 15:20.
2. Roger Martin, *The Design of Business: Why Design Thinking Is the Next Competitive Advantage* (Boston, MA: Harvard Business Press, 2009).
3. I will use the term "apostle" interchangeably with the word "missionary," since both words share the same root meaning ("apostle" being the Greek equivalent of the Latin word "mission"), which is "sent ones."
4. Matt. 25:40.
5. Matt. 6:10.
6. Mark 4:19.
7. I have written about this at length in my book *Life after Church* (Downers Grove, IL: InterVarsity, 2007).

CHAPTER 2

1. Luke 4:18.
2. Mark 2:17.
3. Luke 6:20.
4. Luke 19:10.
5. Acts 11:1–3; 13:1–3.
6. It is in Antioch where Paul spends the most important, most formative years of his life. It is in Antioch where he develops the concept of justification by faith. It is in Antioch where he is taught to plant churches, where he really learns the gospel narrative (all that Jesus said and did) and where he became a redeemed leader. Mark and Luke most likely wrote their gospels in Antioch. Paul takes Mark on his first journey from and returning to Antioch. He finds Luke in his second journey and brings him back to Antioch. Also, in the writing of final first-century church leader Ignatius, the Bishop of Antioch, all of the gospel quotations come from Matthews's gospel, which has led some commentators to contend that Matthew also wrote his gospel in that remarkable community.

CHAPTER 3

1. Vilfredo Pareto, *Manual of Political Economy*, trans. Ann S. Schwier and Alfred N. Page (London: Macmillan, 1971).
2. One notable exception would be John 10. Still, the primary focus of that text is not that we are sheep but that he is a good shepherd. It is a text that seems to be more about the leadership of Jesus than the identity of his followers. The contrast is that the good shepherd lays down his life for his sheep, and the hired hand abandons them when danger comes. Still, the reference is made, and therefore we cannot say it is without value. We should see ourselves as sheep following the good shepherd, while not neglecting the other names he has given us.
3. Matt. 10:16.
4. Matt. 10:1–12, Luke 10:1–23.
5. Shane Hipps, *The Hidden Power of Electronic Culture: How Media*

Shapes Faith, the Gospel, and Church (El Cajon, CA: Youth Specialties, 2006).

6. Acts 3:19.

CHAPTER 4

1. V. David Garrison, *Church Planting Movements: How God is Redeeming a Lost World* (Midlothian, VA: WIGTake Resources, 2004), 16–20.

2. Tom Phillips, "China on Course to Become 'World's Most Christian Nation' within 15 Years," *The Telegraph*, April 19, 2014, http://www .telegraph.co.uk/news/worldnews/asia/china/10776023/China-on -course-to-become-worlds-most-Christian-nation-within-15-years.html.

3. See also Appendix F, which is available at www.underground churchbook.com/appendix.

4. Matt. 28:20.

5. John 6:35–3.

6. If reading this is causing you to ask questions about your own calling, I recommend two resources: Todd Wilson has written an excellent book on the subject called *More* (Grand Rapids: Zondervan, 2016), and we have an online tool you can use at http://callinglab.com.

7. 2 Cor. 4:5.

8. Robert K. Greenleaf and Larry C. Spears, *Servant Leadership: A Journey into the Nature of Legitimate Power and Greatness* (New York: Paulist, 2002), 11.

9. Matt. 20:25–28.

10. Salim Ismail, Michael S. Malone, and Yuri Van Geest, *Exponential Organizations: Why New Organizations Are Ten Times Better, Faster, and Cheaper than Yours (and What to Do about It)* (New York: Diversion, 2014), 37.

11. John 4:35.

12. 2 Cor. 4:7.

CHAPTER 5

1. Matt. 25.

2. Luke 7:22.

3. We do try to assess metrics on the individual level, but it can be difficult to get accurate numbers. Because it is not the ultimate concern for us, we have not worked as hard on these numbers. Still, to give you a sense of it, for every 100 microchurches, we see about 1,000 people engaged in specific mission (as a part of a small living church). In the year of printing, the same 100 microchurches have seen about 460 people come to faith in Jesus, along with countless works of visible mercy, justice, and demonstration of the gospel. So this form of church is strong in both demonstration *and* proclamation of the good news of the kingdom.

4. Luke 12:48.

5. Luke 19:26.

6. Steven Johnson, *Where Good Ideas Come From: The Natural History of Innovation* (New York: Riverhead, 2010).

7. W. Chan Kim and Renée Mauborgne, *Blue Ocean Strategy: How to Create Uncontested Market Space and Make the Competition Irrelevant* (Boston, MA: Harvard Business Review Press, 2016), 2.

8. Jim Tomberlin and Warren Bird, *Better Together: Making Church Mergers Work* (San Francisco: Jossey-Bass, 2012).

9. Based on Tampa Police Department offense records, years 1999 to the end of 2016.

CHAPTER 6

1. Roland Greene, *The Princeton Encyclopedia of Poetry and Poetics*, 4th ed. (Princeton, NJ: Princeton University Press, 2012).

2. "Paradox (literature)," Wikipedia, February 17, 2017, https://en.wikipedia.org/wiki/Paradox_(literature).

3. G. K. Chesterton, *Orthodoxy* (London: John Lane, 1909), 109.

4. Matt. 16:25.

5. Richard Koch, *80/20 Principle and 92 Other Powerful Laws of Nature: The Science of Success* (Boston: Brealey, 2016), ch. 8.

6. Justin Kruger and David Dunning, "Unskilled and Unaware of It: How Difficulties in Recognizing One's Own Incompetence Lead to Inflated Self-Assessments," *Journal of Personality and Social Psychology* 77, no. 6 (1999): 121–34.

7. Ibid.
8. "The root of all virtue and grace, of all faith and acceptable worship, is that we know that we have nothing but what we receive, and bow in deepest humility to wait upon God for it." Andrew Murray, *Humility* (New Kensington, PA: Whitaker, 2005), 13 14.
9. Wystan Hugh Auden and Alan Jacobs, *The Age of Anxiety: A Baroque Eclogue* (Princeton, NJ: Princeton University Press, 2011).
10. Andy Crouch, *Strong and Weak* (Downers Grove, IL: InterVarsity, 2016).
11. Rom. 2:11.
12. Derek Tidball, *The Message of the Cross: Wisdom Unsearchable, Love Indestructible* (Leicester: Inter-Varsity, 2001), 20.
13. Paul Althaus, "Das Kreuz Christi," in *Theologische Aufsätze*, vol. 1 (Gütersloh: Bertelsmann, 1929), 23.
14. John 12:24.
15. Luke 9:23.
16. Tidball, *The Message of the Cross*, 20.

CHAPTER 7

1. We have a team of paid staff who serve the UNDERGROUND as a whole. This team serves the microchurches, their leaders, and the overall work of planting new microchurches in our city and beyond.
2. Karl Barth, *The Word of God and the Word of Man* (Gloucester, MA: P. Smith, 1978), 98.
3. 2 Tim. 3:5.
4. Brené Brown, *Daring Greatly: How the Courage to Be Vulnerable Transforms the Way We Live, Love, Parent, and Lead* (London: Penguin Life, 2015), 117–22.
5. Amos 5:21.
6. Rom. 5:20.
7. Francis Chan and Lisa Chan, *You and Me Forever: Marriage in Light of Eternity* (San Francisco: Claire Love, 2014).
8. Eph. 4:29.

9. Thomas Carlyle, *On Heroes, Hero-worship, and the Heroic in History* (London: Chapman & Hall, 1871), 17.
10. Mark 10:18.
11. Wolfgang Simson, *Houses That Change the World: The Return of the House Churches* (Milton Keynes, UK: Authentic, 2004), 169.

CHAPTER 8

1. You can read the whole document in Appendix A.
2. John P. Kotter, *Leading Change* (Boston: Harvard Business School Press, 1996).
3. 2 Cor. 3:18.
4. Acts 2:17.

WINDOW 2

1. Walter Brueggemann, *Awed to Heaven, Rooted to Earth: Prayers of Walter Brueggemann* (Minneapolis: Fortress, 2003), 31.

CHAPTER 9

1. Matt. 16:18.
2. Eph. 6:10–20.
3. Rev. 19:11–16.
4. John Cassian, *The Works of John Cassian* (Oxford: Parker, 1894), ch. 8.
5. Luke 9:1–2, Matt. 10:5–8.
6. Eph. 6:17, Heb. 4:12.
7. Acts 19:13–16.
8. Eph. 6:12.
9. Phil. 2:3–11.
10. John 3:30.
11. James Davison Hunter, *The Death of Character: Moral Education in an Age without Good or Evil* (New York: Basic Books, 2000).
12. Luke 17:20–21.
13. Ed Stetzer, *Planting Missional Churches* (Nashville: B&H Academic, 2006), 7–8.
14. 2 Cor. 4:5.

CHAPTER 10

1. Isa. 9:7, Luke 1:33, Rev. 11:15.
2. Peter McVerry, *The God of Mercy, the God of the Gospels* (Dublin: Veritas, 2016), 73.
3. Heb. 8:1.
4. John P. Kotter, *Accelerate: Building Strategic Agility for a Faster Moving World* (Boston: Harvard Business Review Press, 2014), vii-viii.
5. Ibid., 134.
6. James 1:2.
7. James 1:3.

CHAPTER 11

1. 2 Cor. 12:9.
2. *Catechism of the Catholic Church*, 1131, http://www.vatican.va/ archive/ccc_css/archive/catechism/p2s1c1a2.htm.
3. 1 Tim. 3:1–13, Titus 1:5–9.
4. Heb. 13.
5. Dee Hock, preface to *Birth of the Chaordic Age* (San Francisco: Berrett-Koehler, 1999).
6. I have included that ordination outline in Appendix D, which is available at www.undergroundchurchbook.com/appendix.
7. See Appendix E, which is available at www.undergroundchurch book.com/appendix.
8. C. S. Lewis, *The Weight of Glory* (New York: Macmillan, 1949), 37.
9. David E. Fitch, *Faithful Presence: Seven Disciplines That Shape the Church for Mission* (Downers Grove, IL: InterVarsity, 2016), 40.
10. Brian Sanders, *In Your Underwear: Life in Intentional Christian Community* (Tampa, FL: Underground Media, 2015), 20–21. See also 2 Cor. 5.
11. John 13.
12. 1 John 1:1.
13. John 1:1–3.
14. John Knox, *The Humanity and Divinity of Christ: A Study of Pattern in Christology* (Cambridge: Cambridge University Press, 1967), 72.

15. John 20:21.
16. Matt. 25:40.

CHAPTER 12

1. Christian Smith, Michael O. Emerson, and Patricia Snell, *Passing the Plate: Why American Christians Don't Give Away More Money* (Oxford: Oxford University Press, 2008), 154.
2. "Church Budget Priorities Study," Christianity Today-Church Law & Tax Group, April 2014, https://static1.squarespace.com/static/53d1217ce4b0d2ee8e81804c/t/54ef5c06e4b0a8822f96d648/1424972806318/Budget+Priorties.pdf.
3. Deut. 15:4.
4. Ralph D. Winter and R. Pierce Beaver, *The Warp and the Woof: Organizing for Mission* (South Pasadena, CA: William Carey Library, 1970), 52–62.
5. John 13:14.
6. Mal. 3:10.
7. Gal. 2:10.
8. Matt. 6:21.

AFTERWORD

1. Acts 1:11.